Curiosities Series

West Virginia CURIOSITIES

Quirky characters, roadside oddities & other offbeat stuff

D1561971

Rick Steelhammer

Guilford, Connecticut

The prices, rates, and hours listed in this guidebook were confirmed at press time. We recommend, however, that you call establishments to obtain current information before traveling.

Photos by Rick Steelhammer unless otherwise noted
Maps by Daniel Lloyd © Rowman & Littlefield
Text design: Bret Kerr
Layout: Mary Ballachino
Project editor: John Burbidge

Library of Congress Cataloging-in-Publication Data

Steelhammer, Rick.
  West Virginia curiosities : quirky characters, roadside oddities & other offbeat stuff / Rick Steelhammer.

    p. cm.
   Includes index.
   ISBN 978-0-7627-4381-0
  1. West Virginia—Guidebooks. 2. West Virginia—Description and travel. 3. Curiosities and wonders—West Virginia. 4. West Virginia—Miscellanea. I. Title.

F239.3.S74 2010
975.4—dc22

                                                                            2009043090

Printed in the United States of America

Distributed by NATIONAL BOOK NETWORK

To my wife, Pam, for putting up with my numerous absences and occasional anxiety attacks during the production of this work; to my daughter, Chelsea, and son, Nick, whom I hope to acquaint with some of the curious new places I've discovered during its compilation; and to the memory of my son, Cody, and the places we managed to explore during our much too brief time together.

iii

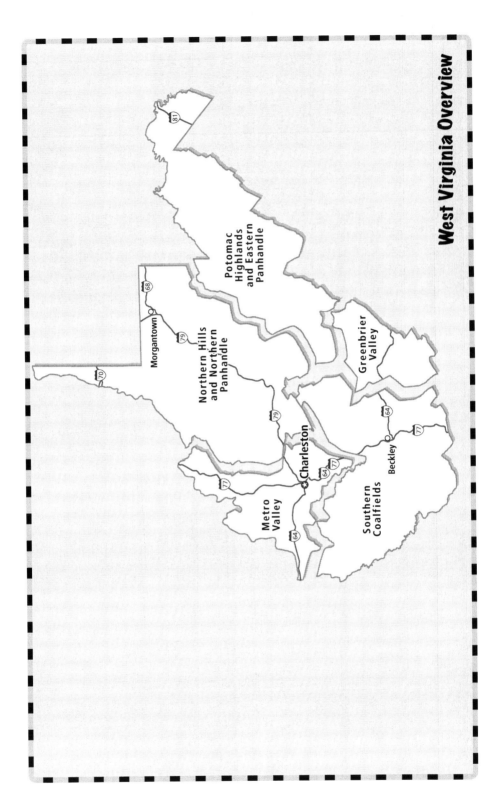

West Virginia Overview

contents

* *

acknowledgments

*Y*ou know you are blessed with good friends when you put out the call for help and are rewarded with more assistance, advice, and encouragement than was ever anticipated. Topping the list were *Charleston Gazette* photographers Larry Pierce and Kenny Kemp, who not only provided numerous images for this guide, but also gave me an extended, confidence-building tutorial on the care and use of the digital camera. Additional photo aid came from the *Gazette*'s Chris Dorst and from state Division of Commerce lens artist Steve Shaluta. Thanks are also in order for state Division of Tourism alumni Caryn Gresham, Matt Turner, and Tony O'Leary for their entry suggestions; the *Gazette*'s Kathy Mobley for solving a variety of technical issues without making me feel more foolish than necessary, and the *Charleston Gazette* for giving me the opportunity to explore the green, rolling hills of West Virginia for more than thirty years—on their dime.

introduction

W est Virginia should be a hard state to stereotype, thousands of hillbilly jokes to the contrary.

It stretches north of Pittsburgh, south of the former Confederate capital of Richmond, as far west as Columbus, and far enough east for its easternmost cities to be included in the Washington, D.C., metropolitan area.

While most of West Virginia lies below the Mason–Dixon line, and the U.S. Census Bureau considers it a southern state, the U.S. Fish and Wildlife Service takes into account its terrain and forest types and includes it in its Northeastern Region.

A jogger using a leisurely pace can travel across West Virginia in less than an hour at Weirton, never leaving the city limits. There, the Ohio and Pennsylvania borders lie only 5 miles apart. On the other hand, a through hiker on the Allegheny Trail, which passes entirely through West Virginia from the Pennsylvania border to the Virginia line, can look forward to 330 miles of mountainous terrain and weeks of heavy legwork before leaving the state.

West Virginia is the only state with two panhandles. The Northern Panhandle ends at the northernmost curve of the Ohio River, 40 miles northwest of Pittsburgh, while the Eastern Panhandle town of Harpers Ferry lies only 50 air miles west of the Washington Monument.

There may be some grounds to support West Virginia's stereotype of being backwoods. Forests cover nearly 80 percent of its terrain, making it the nation's second-most heavily wooded state. And there's certainly no shortage of hills and hollows. West Virginia is the only state that lies entirely within the Appalachian mountain range.

Although rich in natural resources like hardwood timber, coal, and natural gas, the state has one of the nation's lowest per capita income rates. West Virginia has one of the nation's highest home ownership rates, yet corporations—many from outside the state or country—hold the vast tracts of coal and timber property.

introduction

While corporate landowners own the majority of private property in a number of southern counties, West Virginia offers outdoor lovers some of the largest expanses of public land in the East, including one million acres of national forest land.

West Virginia has spawned both down-to-earth "Barney Fife" actor Don Knotts and *The Good Earth* author and Nobel laureate Pearl S. Buck. It's the home state of both John Forbes Nash, the game theory genius of *A Beautiful Mind* fame, and Peter Marshall, the game show host of *Hollywood Squares*.

It's the only state born of the Civil War and the only state to finance its interim government with gold earmarked for construction of an insane asylum that had been taken from a bank at gunpoint by Union troops.

After statehood was established, there was the matter of where to locate the capital. It went from Wheeling in the north to Charleston in the south, then back to Wheeling and back to Charleston. The state's official records spent so much time on riverboats traveling between the two cities that West Virginians joked about having a "Floating Capital."

Then, in 1921, the Capitol Building in downtown Charleston, its top floor loaded with a state police stockpile of small arms ammunition left over from the West Virginia Mine Wars—the largest insurrection since the Civil War—was destroyed by fire. Onlookers had to run for cover when the upstairs ammo cache began to cook off.

A temporary "Pasteboard Capitol" was built in forty-two working days from clapboard and wallboard and served as the seat of government for six years until it, too, went up in flames in 1927. By that time, construction of the current West Virginia Capitol had been authorized, using a design by Cass Gilbert, architect of the U.S. Supreme Court Building in Washington, D.C., and the Woolworth Building in New York. It is widely regarded as one of the nation's most attractive capitol buildings.

introduction

West Virginian sports fans in the Northern Panhandle and northern foothills generally root for professional teams in Pittsburgh, while those in the southern coalfields and Huntington–Charleston metropolitan area are Cincinnati fans—though that's getting harder with each losing season.

It's a state in which Democrats far outnumber Republicans, yet the state voted twice for George W. Bush and elects Republicans as governor nearly as often as Democrats.

West Virginia has one of the nation's highest obesity and lowest exercise rates, yet it offers some of the nation's best hiking, mountain biking, rock climbing, caving, skiing, and whitewater paddling terrain. Even so, Myrtle Beach, South Carolina, is probably West Virginians' most popular vacation destination.

West Virginia is currently the state with the fewest foreign-born residents, but it was once teeming with immigrants who named dozens of small towns here in honor of their homelands. It would make for a long day's drive, but in West Virginia, it's possible to go to Berlin, Cuba, Congo, London, Glasgow, Ottawa, Yukon, Vienna, Ireland, Burma, Rangoon, Cairo, Palestine, Shanghai, and Porto (as it's spelled here) Rico in a single day. And there would still be time to drive to Rocket Center in Mineral County and prepare for road trips to Venus, Sun, Pluto, Vulcan, and Red Star.

It's a patriotic, friendly, church-going state with a bit of a chip on its shoulder for often being characterized as more rustic than it really is—and for still being mistakenly considered a part of Virginia. That said, if you visit here, you will be welcome and won't be a stranger for long.

Just don't tell your new West Virginia friends about your cousin in Richmond and wonder aloud if they might know him.

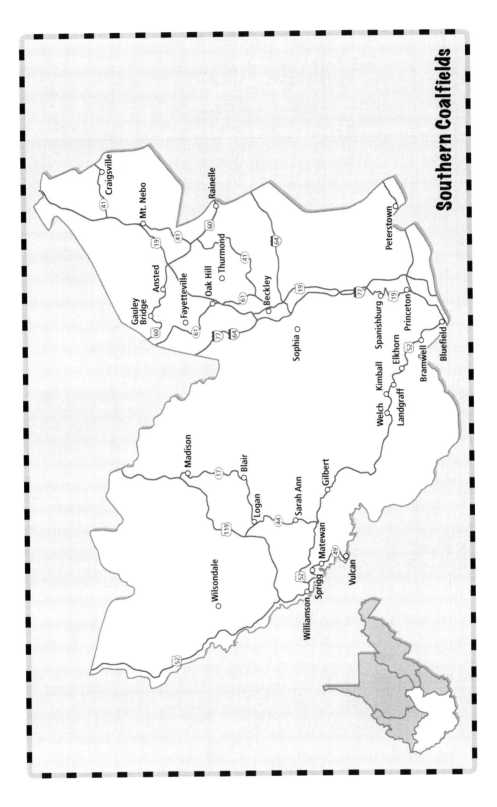

Southern Coalfields

1

Southern Coalfields

C oal is still king across much of southern West Virginia, fueling the economy with good wages and tax receipts, while altering the landscape in ways that were barely imaginable a century ago. In areas where the coal reserves are played out, the towns are smaller, but nature is healing the landscape, creating new opportunities for jobs and recreation for those who remain.

Trout have returned to a number of once-polluted streams, and ATV riders and off-road motorcyclists come here to ride the traces of haul roads once used for mining and timbering.

The region's steep mountains and pounding whitewater provide ways for people who work hard to play equally hard. It's the home of the only bridge in the country where, one day a year, it's legal to climb over the rail and parachute off.

History here is no Disney movie—it's written in blood. By the time the Hatfield–McCoy feud was winding down and the Matewan Massacre was over, federal troops and Army Air Corps bombers were facing down an army of well-armed coal miners atop Blair Mountain in the largest insurrection since the Civil War.

But it's also a whimsical place, where gravity is challenged by descending into the Mystery Hole at Ansted and where you can park your bus on a rock in the middle of the river and use it for a fishing camp at Gauley Bridge. And if it's good enough for Gilligan of Gilligan's Island to retire to, it's good enough for me.

Gravity's Cavity
Ansted

First-time visitors to the Mystery Hole don't really know what to expect when they pull into the roadside attraction's parking area off US 60, on a bluff overlooking the New River Gorge near the town of Ansted. There, they are confronted by a military-style Quonset hut painted in psychedelic colors with a vintage Volkswagen bug, decorated in hippie colors and decals, protruding from its side. Atop the building, a huge fiberglass gorilla crouches and glowers before a row of American flags.

Gravity is seemingly defied in the pit beneath this Volkswagen-impaled Quonset hut.

Opened in 1972 by local entrepreneur Donald Wilson, whose cheerful line of hokey background info on the Mystery Hole's "powers" was alone worth the price of admission, the attraction temporarily closed following Wilson's death in 1998. Michiganders Will and Sandy Morrison bought Wilson's business in 1999 and have kept many of Wilson's narrative remarks as part of their tour repertoire.

Just outside the Quonset hut gift shop and ticket office, a stairway leads down into Mystery Hole itself. On the descent, signs carry a series of warnings ranging from NOT RESPONSIBLE FOR ACCIDENTS OR AFTER-EFFECTS to PEOPLE WITH HIGH BLOOD PRESSURE OR HEART AILMENT DO NOT ENTER! and SHOES RECOMMENDED FOR TOUR.

Once inside the Hole, tour guides demonstrate a variety of gravity-defying feats, such as balls rolling up a series of ramps, people sitting in chairs that seem to cling unsupported to a wall, and fellow visitors walking at a forty-five-degree slant.

The experience is generally in keeping with a posted claim that NATURE'S GRAVITY SEEMS TO HAVE GONE HAYWIRE, AND YOUR SENSE OF BALANCE IS EXTREMELY UPSET. The Mystery Hole is open April through October but closed on Tuesday. For information on operating hours and admission fees, call (304) 658-9101, or visit www.mysteryhole.com.

Underground Railroad
Beckley

Visitors who come to the Beckley Exhibition Coal Mine hoping to learn a little about what the life of a coal miner is like get the shaft—a 1,500-foot deep, 6-foot high, and 10-foot-wide shaft, to be precise.

The Exhibition Coal Mine is one of the few places anywhere in which the public is able to safely and legally see the inside of an underground coal mine. The attraction came into being by accident, after workers building Beckley's New River Park during the 1960s inadvertently uncovered a portion of the shaft. Rather than reseal and forget the old mine passage, city officials decided to reopen the mine to tourists.

Mining the tourist economy in Beckley is the Exhibition Coal Mine.

Visitors ride "man cars," or low-slung, open-topped railcars deep into the mine, which produced coal from 1890 to 1910. Guides on the hourlong trip are retired miners who, at stops along the shaft, explain or demonstrate bygone mining techniques, like using hand-powered augers to drill blast holes in the mine face, so that coal could be shot out of the 3-foot seam and hand-loaded into carts. While the coal was only 3 feet thick, the shaft was made higher to accommodate the horses and oxen used to pull wagons of coal out of the mine.

The guides also point out widow-making "kettlebottoms," the petrified tree trunks that occasionally fall from mine roofs with enough force to kill anyone below, and talk about "black damp," or potentially lethal pockets of oxygen-deficient air sometimes found in sections of underground mines. Then there are "mountain bumps" and "rib rolls" in which rocks are expelled from the walls of mine shafts due to earth slips, methane explosions, and roof falls. The exhibition is inspected daily for safety by its trained crew of guides. More than 50,000 people a year have toured the mine with no problems more severe than the occasional case of claustrophobia. The mine stays a constant 50 degrees Fahrenheit, even in deepest, steamiest summer, so bring a light jacket.

Outside the mine, there is a restored coal camp and a large new company store building, housing a museum and gift shop—scrip not accepted, these days.

The Exhibition Coal Mine is open April through November. Call (304) 256-1747, or visit www.beckleymine.com.

Bombs over . . . West Virginia?

Blair Mountain

If you were a union-loving coal miner in West Virginia in 1921, you weren't the least bit paranoid if you thought the government was out to get you. It was.

Those fighting for recognition by the United Mine Workers of America during the era of the West Virginia Mine Wars not only were charged with treason but also faced armed threats from sheriffs' deputies and their hired guns, the state police, the National Guard, regular Army troops—even bombers manned by the Army Air Corps.

Military aviation legend Billy Mitchell was ordered to fly his armed and loaded Eighty-eighth Light Bomber Squadron to Charleston to assist the government effort from a higher plane. Luckily for the miners, cooler heads eventually prevailed (or Mitchell's tear gas ordnance malfunctioned, according to other accounts), and the World War I flying hero never got the chance to use his fourteen aircraft to bomb his countrymen, as he appeared anxious to do, according to press reports at the time.

Mitchell's air crews had to stand down in August 1921, when an army of more than 5,000 miners marched on a force of about 2,000

Cross Country

If you drive down any major West Virginia highway, keep an eye out for hillside clearings, ridgetop pastures, or intriguing rock formations; chances are better than even that within thirty minutes you will encounter a cluster of Coffindaffer crosses.

Depending on one's point of view, they are considered either spiritual eye openers or scenic eyesores. But they've been around long enough in West Virginia that they have become an everyday part of the rural landscape.

More than 1,800 crosses were erected by a Craigsville oil driller. Kenny Kemp

The 20-foot-tall trios of pole-built crosses—the middle one gold flanked by two painted baby blue—are the product of Bernard L. Coffindaffer, an oil driller, coal-washing plant operator, and country minister from Craigsville in Nicholas County. In 1984, while resting at home following a heart bypass operation, Coffindaffer reported having a vision in which the spirit of God told him to build crosses in all fifty states, starting with West Virginia. The World War II Marine Corps veteran promptly sold his substantial business holdings and founded the nonprofit Crosses of Mercy–Cast Thy Bread, Inc.

Starting in September 1984, Coffindaffer began erecting cross clusters on the property of like-minded landowners across the state in his quest to get passersby to remember Christ's sacrifice and prepare for His return. At the peak of his mission, he had seven full-time work crews scouting out sites, making arrangements with property owners, and erecting the cross clusters. That work extended beyond West Virginia's borders to include twenty-eight other states, as well as the District of Columbia, Zambia, and the Philippines.

By the time Coffindaffer died of a heart attack in his home in 1993, he had erected 1,864 cross clusters, spending about $3 million in the effort.

★ ★

Nicholas County residents gather near the crash site of one of General Billy Mitchell's Martin bombers, deployed during the 1921 Battle of Blair Mountain. West Virginia Archives

sheriffs' deputies, hired thugs, and private detective personnel dug in on Blair Mountain, on the border separating Boone and Logan counties.

After skirmishing on the mountain claimed the lives of fewer than fifty combatants—most of them UMWA supporters—the miners, many who had recently served in the Army during World War I, refused to take up arms against the federal troops who arrived on the scene and surrendered peacefully.

A few days later, one of Mitchell's Martin bombers flew into a storm en route to Langley Field in Virginia and crashed into a hillside near Drennen in Nicholas County, killing all but one member of the crew. Several area residents still own pieces of the bomber. The wreck site is believed to have been obliterated when a surface mine opened in the Drennen area decades after the crash.

Bluefield Brain
Bluefield

In the early 1940s, while other kids in the Mercer County town of Bluefield were playing catch, riding bikes, or hanging out with their friends, John Forbes Nash was likely to be at home, leafing through *Compton's Pictured Encyclopedia,* or building a radio from spare parts.

The son of an electrical engineer for Appalachian Power and a former English teacher who graduated from West Virginia University at

He's got game theory: Nobel laureate John Forbes Nash grew up in this tiny Bluefield home.

★ ★

the age of sixteen, Nash showed few obvious signs of having a beautiful mind early in his life. He worked as an advertising supplement inserter at the *Bluefield Daily Telegraph,* read *Time* and *Life* magazines from cover to cover, and conducted electrical and chemical experiments in his bedroom. But his classroom performance was deemed to be a bit underwhelming until his final years of high school.

Bluefield, he recalled in a 1994 autobiographical sketch, "was not a community of scholars or of high technology. . . . So, from [an] intellectual viewpoint, it offered the sort of challenge that one had to learn from the world's knowledge rather than from the knowledge of the immediate community."

Nash absorbed what he could from the town. As a high school student, he took mathematics courses at Bluefield College. With his father, he coauthored the article "Sag and Tension Calculations for Cable and Wire Spans Using Catenary Formulas," which probably did little to win friends and earn dates, but it did appear in the professional journal *Electrical Engineering.*

He attended Carnegie Tech, now Carnegie Mellon University, on a full scholarship, earning both his bachelor's and master's degrees in 1948 at the age of twenty. His subsequent involvement with a Navy research project, his groundbreaking work on game theory and differential geometry, his earning of the Nobel Prize for Economics in 1994, and his bouts with and eventual victory over schizophrenia were the subject of Sylvia Nasar's biography *A Beautiful Mind.* A movie by the same name loosely based on Nasar's book, starring Russell Crowe as Nash, was nominated for eight Oscars following its release in 2001.

Sweat and Sour
Bluefield

Perched on a 2,600-foot-high plateau in the shadow of East River Mountain, the Mercer County town of Bluefield bills itself as "Nature's Air-Conditioned City," a cool place to chill out when sweltering temperatures sweep through the lowlands. In an effort to cash

Heat waves are so rare in Bluefield that town officials pour free lemonade when the mercury reaches 90.

in on the town's heat-beating image, the Bluefield Chamber of Commerce has made it a practice to serve free lemonade on the rare occasions that temperatures surpass the 90-degree mark.

Since the town's free lemonade days began in 1939, there have been at least thirty-four summers in which the services of the town's "Lemonade Lassies," the volunteers who serve up the pucker-producing coolant, have not been needed. From 1960 to 1982, free lemonade was dispensed only once. However, the summer of 2007 made up for many of the lemonade-free years, producing a record eighteen days with temperatures 90 degrees or hotter. Whether or not it reaches 90, Bluefield celebrates Lemonade Days each year in late July with street fairs, music, entertainment, and free lemonade.

For more information, call the Mercer County Convention and Visitors Bureau at (304) 325-8438, or visit www.mccvb.com.

Town with a Rich History

Bramwell

Sure, millionaires may be as common as caviar in places like Beverly Hills, Palm Springs, and Aspen, but in tiny Bramwell, they were once so abundant that the team name for Bramwell High School athletes was the Millionaires, and someone with a seven-figure income lived on virtually every block.

The Mercer County town that lies along a horseshoe bend of the Bluestone River is credited with having had America's densest per capital population of millionaires, in an era when $1 million bought a lot more than a vacation condo in the Hamptons or a couple of Porsche Carrera GTs.

The town's wealth can be traced to the discovery of the rich Pocahontas Coalfield, with seams measuring up to 13 feet thick, which

Millionaires were once a dime a dozen—well, nineteen for every four thousand citizens—in this southern coalfield town. Kenny Kemp

spurred a stampede of coal operators, miners, developers, and entrepreneurs into Mercer and McDowell counties. Among them was the New York civil engineer Joseph Bramwell, who gave his name to the tiny community where he had been assigned to serve as postmaster. By 1885, streets had been laid out, and Bramwell's attractive riverside setting had been divided into lots for homes, attracting newly arrived coal company officials. Soon the town became known as a haven for the area's have-it-alls.

At least fourteen millionaires made Bramwell their home by 1900. Their Victorian trophy homes featured indoor pools, copper roofs, and walls of English brick and Italian masonry. Fourteen passenger trains made daily stops at the wealthy town's depot, off-loading imported home furnishings, gourmet foods, and consumer luxury items. At the end of the 1800s, it was the only American city outside New York where Chanel No. 5 perfume was sold, and the town's Bryant Newbold Pharmacy sold about $25,000 worth of the fragrance a year.

Bramwell, believed to be the first U.S. city to make use of electric streetlights, had its own water, electric, and telephone companies operating by the opening years of the twentieth century.

The Great Depression sent Bramwell's millionaires into exile, along with most of its less-wealthy residents. Only about 400 people now remain in the town that once had a population nearly ten times as large. But nearly all of the millionaires' homes remain intact and are lovingly cared for by their new owners, most of whom make their houses available for tours in May and December. The town's train station has been converted into a museum, offering visitors a glimpse of Bramwell in its heyday. Bramwell is located about 8 miles north of Bluefield on US 52. For more information, visit the Mercer County Convention and Visitors Bureau at www.mccvb.com, or call (304) 325-8438.

★ ★

Trout among the Trash

Elkhorn

It wasn't God who made Elkhorn Creek one of West Virginia's most productive trout streams—at least not directly.

It was a roadside mishap that converted the once-dead McDowell County stream into what is perhaps the state's top producer of citation-size rainbow and brown trout.

Severely polluted by discharges from coal-cleaning plants in the 1950s and early 1960s, Elkhorn was known mainly as a local sewage collection system and the source of devastating floods until its reputation took a turn for the better in the early 1970s. It was then that a trout hatchery truck broke down on US 52, which follows the stream from its source near the Mercer County line 20 miles north into the

Nelson Sorah casts for trout in Elkhorn Creek. Lawrence Pierce

town of Welch, where it flows into the Guyandotte River. With no other trout tankers available to offload the disabled hatchery vehicle, its driver decided the load of rainbow trout he was hauling stood a slightly better chance of surviving in the creek than they did on the side of the road.

As it turned out, the trout not only survived, they flourished and multiplied. After local anglers discovered the presence of hook-jawed, salmon-sized rainbows in their stream, biologists with the Division of Natural Resources decided to see if they could tweak the accidental trophy trout formula even more. In 1993, they introduced an experimental stocking of brown trout into Elkhorn.

These days, Elkhorn Creek is one of the very few West Virginia streams in which rainbow and brown trout, both nonnative species, spawn and naturally reproduce. Catches in the 4- to 5-pound range are not uncommon. An 11-pound, 2-ounce rainbow reeled in at the town of Kimball broke a state record that had stood for thirty-three years. Experienced Elkhorn Creek anglers routinely catch more than a dozen trout an hour.

But dining on the Elkhorn Creek trout is another matter, even though the catch-and-release ethic is not legally enforced.

While cold water seeping into its headwaters from played-out coal mines keeps the stream cool and flowing steady year-round, untreated sewage discharged into Elkhorn from downstream coal towns keeps it full of bacterial contaminants. The DNR advises anglers not to eat Elkhorn Creek trout, who owe much of their high growth rate to the nutrients they take in from sewage outflows.

Since the stream winds its way through a series of coal towns on its way to Welch, anglers face other unusual challenges, like encountering discarded appliances, junk cars, and mean dogs.

"A buddy of mine caught a nice rainbow from under an old mattress," said Kevin Adkins of Charleston, while taking part in a Trout Unlimited cleanup of the stream, which cleared sixty-eight bags of trash from a ½-mile stretch.

★ ★

Ah, Chute!
Fayetteville

When fall colors reach their peak in the federally protected New River Gorge canyon country near Fayetteville, it creates scenery to die for.

But that's not the main reason hundreds of people from around the world gather at the New River Gorge Bridge each year on the third Saturday of October and take a flying leap off the 876-foot-high span.

The third Saturday of October is Bridge Day, a festival commemorating the completion of the world's second-longest arch bridge back in 1977. The highlight of the annual fall festival is the almost nonstop six-hour parade of parachutists jumping from a platform above the bridge deck and making the drop to the tiny shoreline landing zone

On the third Saturday of October, parachutists from around the world plunge into the fall colors surrounding the New River Gorge Bridge. Chris Dorst

below. If everything goes according to plan, the trip takes about twenty seconds, and there's time to catch a shuttle back to the bridge for repeat jumps. If not, the day ends abruptly in a fraction over eight seconds.

Bridge Day is the world's biggest event for BASE jumpers—those who travel by parachute from buildings, antennae, spans, or earth—drawn to the year's only legal day of BASE jumping, provided in conjunction with well-trained shoreline and midstream rescue crews and shuttle services. The bridge is also opened to pedestrians, and as many as 180,000 have been known to gather on or near the span to watch jumpers, often clad in colorful, comical costumes, make their leaps of faith into the gorge, which is a unit of the National Park Service.

Other high-adrenaline activities, such as rappelling and riding zip lines off the span, also take place on Bridge Day. The BASE jumping component of the celebration began with five participants in 1980 and now draws 450 or more annually.

The New River Gorge Bridge, featured on West Virginia's quarter, lies about 3 miles north of Fayetteville on US 19. For more information, visit the Fayette County Chamber of Commerce Web site at www.fayettecounty.com, or call (304) 465-5617.

Busman's Holiday
Gauley Bridge

When Walter "Bruiser" Cole wants to get away from it all, he climbs aboard his vintage Greyhound bus, sits back, and watches the river flow past his windows.

That's easy to do when your bus is perched on your own private island in a mile-long pool of calm water that surrounds the point where the Gauley River flows into the New River to form the Kanawha.

Cole had the bus, which he bought in 1954, towed to the Fayette County town of Gauley Bridge, then had it barged a few hundred yards cross-river to his tiny, boulder-strewn island, where he winched

One man's decommissioned bus is another man's
island getaway in West Virginia's New River.

it into place above the high water mark. He converted the bus into
a fishing camp and added a porch, boat dock, handrails, electrical
hookups, running water, and a flagpole to complete his island retreat.

The bus-topped island, often displaying Cole's large American
flag, is clearly visible from US 60 and the town of Gauley Bridge. It
has been the topic of speculation for decades, and a number of leg-
ends have sprung up regarding how the passenger vehicle arrived on
its water-surrounded perch. One common folktale is that it washed
down the New River during a flood and came to rest at its current
location by chance.

During the 1970s, A. James Manchin, the uncle of current governor Joe Manchin, vowed to remove the bus from the island in his
capacity as head of an aggressive new state cleanup program that
targeted abandoned vehicles. When Manchin found out the bus was
a vacation home, he moved on to rustier pastures.

Home on the Driving Range

Gilbert

Wild horses may not be able to drag you away from a long-awaited round of golf at Twisted Gun Golf Course near Gilbert in Mingo County, but they could distract you from sinking a putt.

One of West Virginia's newest courses, Twisted Gun is built on a reclaimed surface mine surrounded by a vast tract of corporate land stretching to the Kentucky border. On a series of ridges adjacent to the golf course, more than seventy-five feral, or free-running, horses roam dozens of square miles of open country, including thousands of acres of grassy, sparsely forested reclaimed strip mines, and gas line rights-of-way.

County officials say free-running horses have been fending for themselves in the wide-open spaces for ten or more years, after being

Free-running horses put the west in West Virginia near the Twisted Gun Golf Course. Lawrence Pierce

turned loose to graze on the corporate rangeland by their owners or escaping from farm enclosures. Employees at Twisted Gun say the mustang wannabes occasionally wander onto the fairways to graze on greener grass—and put major divots in the fairways.

Coal truck drivers and gas well maintenance crews say the horses seem to be divided into four herds, including one that numbers about fifty. A few goats and mules have also been spotted grazing on the open rangeland.

While the free-running horses are putting the "west" in today's West Virginia, the Horsepen Mountain end of their range was once used as a place to gather horses stolen from settlers in the mid-1700s. Aracoma, daughter of Chief Cornstalk of the Shawnee, and her husband, Bolling Baker, a white "longhunter" who made prolonged scouting and hunting trips through the frontier, directed the used-horse operation at Horsepen.

Tale of the Trail
Gilbert

While it may be named for the famed feuding families who populated the hills and hollows through which it winds, the Hatfield–McCoy Trail system and the towns it passes through are earning a reputation for hospitality among the ATV riders and off-road motorcyclists who use it.

Totaling 500 miles in six southern West Virginia counties in 2009 with plans to expand to 2,000 miles in nine counties, the Hatfield–McCoy network is the biggest and best-known off-road vehicle trail east of the Mississippi. It is divided into a series of six separate trail systems—Little Coal River, Bearwallow, Buffalo Mountain, Rockhouse, Pinnacle Creek, and Indian Ridge—each served by its own trailhead facility. Spur trails lead from the trail loops into several southern West Virginia towns, where laws have been enacted allowing ATVs and other off-road vehicles to operate on city streets. This allows riders to drive directly into communities such as Gilbert, Matewan, Man, and Delbarton for food, fuel, repairs, and lodging.

ATV riders head out for a day's ride on the largest off-road trail system in the East. Lawrence Pierce

While trails in the system are designed to meet federal Bureau of Land Management standards, the Hatfield–McCoy passes exclusively through private property owned by large coal and land-holding companies, thanks to use and liability agreements with the Hatfield–McCoy Trail Authority. Eastern riders hungry for backcountry pump millions of dollars annually into the local economy.

Plans call for the Hatfield–McCoy trail to expand into several more southern counties and for trails to be built directly linking several of the systems together. For details, call (800) 592-2217, or visit www.trailsheaven.com.

Monumental Effort

Kimball

After crumbling from neglect in the 1980s and being gutted by fire in 1991, the nation's first and only monument to the 400,000 African Americans who served in World War I proved to be as tough and enduring as the men it was built to honor.

Construction of the three-story, Greek-style Kimball War Memorial Building was authorized by the McDowell County Commission in 1924, in response to a petition by a group representing the 1,500 black residents of the county who served in the War to End All Wars. The architect Hassel T. Hicks of Welch, West Virginia, designed the building, which was completed in 1927 on a hillside overlooking the coal town of Kimball.

Tiny Kimball is home to the nation's first memorial to black World War I vets.

Skeleton in Her Closet

Say the word *slalom* or *luge* in southern West Virginia, and people may think you're talking about a large fish or something that's best spit, rather than swallowed.

Winter Olympics sports may not get a lot of attention in these parts, but Logan native Lee Ann Parsley didn't let that stop her from making a meteoric rise to the top in the international sport of skeleton ice sledding.

A graduate of Marshall University in Huntington, where she played basketball from 1986 to 1990, scoring more than 1,000 points during her collegiate career, Parsley went on to become a nurse, firefighter, and Olympic skeleton medalist. She took up the sport in 1998, enrolling in a skeleton class at Park City, Utah, during a break from duties as a firefighter in Ohio. By 1999 she had become the first American woman to win a World Cup medal in skeleton, with a second-place finish in Norway. Parsley finished fourth in the 2000 Goodwill Games, then took part in the 2002 Winter Olympics in Salt Lake City. There, she was one of eight U.S. team members to carry the flag from the World Trade Center during the opening ceremonies, then slid her way to a silver medal in the skeleton event, one-tenth of a second behind teammate Tristan Gale.

Parsley, the national champion in her sport in 2004, was trying to earn a spot on the 2006 Olympic team during a competition in Calgary, Alberta, in 2005 when she was struck by a runaway bobsled. She suffered a leg injury and was unable to compete at full capacity during team trials seventy-two hours after the accident. While she didn't make the 2006 Olympic team as an athlete, she did participate as a coach in the skeleton event.

Designed to serve as a community center and meeting place as well as a World War I memorial, the building was used to host high school proms, reunions, and wedding receptions for people of all races. Cab Calloway and Count Basie are among the musicians who have performed in the Memorial's small auditorium. In its early years, it was the meeting place for West Virginia's first all-black American Legion post, named in honor of Luther Patterson, the first black soldier from McDowell County to be killed in the war.

In the early 1990s, the McDowell County Museum Commission took on the task of raising more than $1 million to stabilize and repair the building. In 2007 the completed work on the restored building was cited as a "preservation solution" by the National Trust for Historic Preservation.

Room with a Choo
Landgraff

For some people, the sound of coal trains rumbling right past the bedroom window several times a night could make for a hellish experience. For others, it would be music to the ears.

It's the latter group of people the operators of the Elkhorn Inn aim to please. Dan and Elisse Clark came across the former Empire Coal & Coke Clubhouse in 2002 while working for the Federal Emergency Management Agency following heavy flooding in McDowell County in 2001 and 2002.

The building wasn't hard to spot, since it was virtually the only structure left standing in the tiny coal town of Landgraff following the floods. Plus, there was a replica of Shakespeare's Globe Theater still mostly standing out back. Billie Jean Cherry, a former banking executive and mayor of the nearby town of Keystone, had partially converted the mine company clubhouse into a bed-and-breakfast lodge with a community theater component before the floods swept through. At about the same time, Cherry was also swept up in a federal fraud and money laundering case involving more than $4 million

The day-and-night sound of coal trains passing is music to the ears of rail fans from around the world at the Elkhorn Inn. Lawrence Pierce

in missing bank funds that netted a sixteen-year sentence in federal prison.

The Clarks envisioned refurbishing the clubhouse as a getaway for guests interested in escaping the urban rat race and perhaps taking advantage of the trout-teeming waters of Elkhorn Creek, which flows past the inn. But their first night in the restored building convinced them they should try reaching out to rail buffs. "The whole building shook when the trains came by," Elisse recalled. "We clutched each other and said, 'We've got to find people who love trains.'"

They did.

The home page for the inn's Web site (www.elkhorninnwv.com) features a photo of a coal train rolling past the restored three-story brick building, as well as a promotion for its special train-view guest rooms and locomotive-viewing balcony. Rail fans from around the

Clogging in His Arteries

From dancing on a doghouse roof in the 1991 PBS documentary *Dancing Outlaw* to dancing onstage to "Louisiana Stripes" with Hank Williams III in 2008, it's been a long, strange trip for mountain dancing cult figure and Boone County native Jesco White.

The son of backwoods dance impresario D. Ray White, who was himself the subject of a PBS documentary, Mike Seeger's 1989 *Talking Feet*, Jesse "Jesco" White has danced to the beat of a different drummer since his formative years in the Boone County coal community of Bandytown, where he was born in 1956.

His unique blend of tap and clog dancing was discovered by documentary filmmaker Jacob Young, who initially intended to shoot a follow-up piece on Jesco's father, only to discover that D. Ray White had recently been murdered. *Dancing Outlaw* covered not only Jesco White's dancing skill, but his struggles with poverty, drug abuse, personal relationships, and isolation.

Among those who saw *Dancing Outlaw* was the comedian Tom Arnold, who invited White to appear on an episode of *Roseanne*, which starred Arnold's then-wife, Roseanne Barr. White's trip to Hollywood and appearance on the show were the subject of a second PBS documentary by Jacob Young, *Dancing Outlaw II: Jesco Goes to Hollywood.*

A new documentary about White and his family, *The Wild and Wonderful Whites of West Virginia*, produced by Johnny Knoxville, was released by MTV Studios in 2009, following a debut at the Tribeca Film Festival in New York. According to the film's official plot synopsis (available at www.jackassworld.com), the movie covers "shootouts, robberies, gas huffing, drug dealing, pill popping, murders and tap dancing." Meanwhile, Jesco White continues to dance, has taken up the cigar box banjo, and has had a bobble-head doll made in his image.

White is mentioned in recent songs recorded by Big and Rich, the Kentucky Headhunters, Hank Williams III, and Ekoostik Hookah. A short clip of him dancing is included in Beck's music video "Loser."

world visit the hotel just to be in close proximity to the busy Norfolk & Southern tracks and the coal trains that rumble down them.

"There may be no better legal location from which to watch, photograph and film trains in America," gushed a reviewer in *Railroad & Railfan* magazine.

The Elkhorn Inn is located on US 52, about 20 miles north of Bluefield. Call (800) 708-2040.

War in the Streets
Matewan

Across the street from the post office in the Tug River Valley town of Matewan, four bullet holes form a neat pattern in the brick wall of the building that once housed the Bank of Matewan. The deeply gouged holes, marked with brass plugs and a historic plaque, account for only four of the hundreds of rounds of hot lead that flew through the air, buildings, and bodies here in May 1920, during the Matewan Massacre—the opening volley of what was to become the West Virginia Mine Wars.

In the spring of 1920, a nationwide coal strike had recently been settled, giving union miners a 27 percent pay raise and making organization all the more attractive to the nonunionized miners in southern West Virginia. To discourage miners in the Matewan area from organizing, coal operators employed hired guns from the Baldwin-Felts Detective Agency to evict miners who signed union cards from their company-owned houses. On May 19, the No. 29 train from Bluefield brought a squad of Baldwin-Felts operatives to Matewan, to clear out union sympathizers from a coal camp on the outskirts of town. Six families were pulled from their homes and all their possessions piled up in the street before the police chief of Matewan, Sid Hatfield, and Mayor C. C. Testerman, backed by a group of armed miners and townspeople, decided to intervene. A confrontation took shape in downtown Matewan, as the police chief and mayor and their supporters squared off with Albert Felts and his group of heavily

Bullet holes pock the wall of the old Bank of Matewan building, where a shootout in 1920 left ten coal company detectives, two miners, and Matewan's mayor dead. Kenny Kemp

armed detectives, and each party threatened to arrest the other. History is not clear about who shot first, but Testerman and Felts were the first to be brought down in a brief but deadly hail of gunfire that killed seven detectives, two miners, and Mayor Testerman.

Hatfield was tried and acquitted for his role in the deaths. But the following summer in nearby Welch, he and a friend, Ed Chambers, were assassinated in front of their wives by Baldwin-Felts detectives as they approached the steps of the McDowell County Courthouse. No one was ever arrested or charged for their murder. The killings of Hatfield and Chambers galvanized the spirit of thousands of union miners, who grabbed rifles and pistols and moved as an army into the nonunion stronghold of Logan County to take part in the Battle of Blair Mountain, the largest armed insurrection since the Civil War (see "Bombs Over . . . West Virginia?").

Matewan remains a coal town, but its economy is beginning to diversify thanks in large part to its direct link to the Hatfield–McCoy Trail system, the largest trail network for ATVs and off-road motorcycles in the East (see "Tale of the Trail"). Laws have been enacted

Felonious Flag Waving

The flag ownership rate in West Virginia is probably well above the national average, but a peculiar state law still on the books prohibits owning or displaying a red flag, black flag, or any other flag that shows sympathy "to institutions or forms of government hostile, inimical, or antagonistic to the form or spirit of the constitution of the state or of the United States."

Somehow, word hasn't gotten out to the state's roadside Confederate flag vendors, who would seem to be covered by the last two lines of the law.

The prohibition against red flags and black flags presumably had something to do with the state's desire to discourage communism/socialism and anarchism. It probably dates to the West Virginia Mine Wars days, when outside agitators were believed to have been plotting in every hollow. These days, the black flag is better known as the clear-the-track symbol for stock car racing or the background for POW/MIA supporters' flags.

★ ★

allowing ATV operators to drive directly off the trail and into town to take in meals, lodging, fuel, and repairs, as well as a little history. The 1987 John Sayles movie *Matewan,* starring Chris Cooper and James Earl Jones, was based on the Matewan Massacre but was actually filmed in the New River Gorge town of Thurmond.

For more information on Matewan, past and present, visit www .matewan.com.

A Place to Get Plowed
Mount Nebo

Back in 2004, when Steve and Joyce Brown's Mount Nebo Farm Equipment dealership fell behind on payments to the bank, and foreclosure was moving from the conceptual stage toward reality, a friend jokingly suggested converting the tractor store into a bar. But

Plant yourself at the bar at this former tractor dealership.

after selling their tools to keep the suits at bay for a few months, the more the Browns thought about becoming bar owners, the less it felt like a joke. They converted the office and parts department into a kitchen and walk-in cooler, transformed the showroom into a bar-room, covered the walls with rough-cut boards, built a bar, and fab-ricated bar stools from tractor seats and pipe. A rusty 1919 Fordson hand-cranked, steel-wheeled tractor that had been shading weeds in a field behind the dealership was cleaned and painted, pulled into the barroom, and surrounded with pool tables. Old tools and farm equip-ment that had been lying around the dealership were hung on the walls. As their planned grand opening date approached, the Browns sank the last of their cash into licensing fees and a cache of beer. Friends chipped in to buy enough liquor to get the Mount Nebo Trac-tor Bar rolling.

Since then, the Tractor Bar has become a popular watering hole among locals, white-water paddlers in the area to run the nearby New and Gauley rivers, bikers, and probably more than a few tractor fanatics. It has become one of the area's strongest supporters of live performance music, hosting both weekend and midweek shows.

The Tractor Bar is located about 1 mile off the WV 41/Mount Nebo exit of four-lane US 19, about 5 miles south of Summersville. For information, call (304) 872-8100, or visit www.tractorbar.com.

End of the Lonesome Highway
Oak Hill

When country music legend Hank Williams boarded his blue Cadillac and hit the road in Montgomery, Alabama, on December 28, 1952, he hoped he was setting out on the comeback trail. It turned out he was on the road to ruin, and its last exit was Oak Hill, West Virginia.

Fired from the Grand Ole Opry for missing show dates and demoted to the *Louisiana Hayride,* the Opry's radio farm club, Wil-liams was scheduled to begin a series of major road performances, starting with a New Year's Eve show costarring comedians Homer

Official Sloth

In March 2008 the West Virginia Legislature became the first governing body in the nation to officially approve of sloth—or at least one prehistoric form of sloth.

The story behind the slothful legislation dates to the mid-1790s, when frontiersmen extracting saltpeter from Haynes Cave in Monroe County came across the fossilized bones of a large animal with huge claws. Intrigued with their find, the men dug up the bones and took them to the Monticello home of Thomas Jefferson, an amateur paleontologist as well as a planter, who was soon to become John Adams's vice president.

Impressed with the animal's ferocious-looking claws, Jefferson hypothesized that the bones came from some type of lionlike cat. In 1797, when he presented the fossilized remains at the annual meeting of the American Philosophical Society, of which he was president, he called the animal *Megalonyx*, Latin for "giant claw." Two years later Caspar Wistar, the chairman of the anatomy department at the University of Pennsylvania, determined that the bones actually belonged to a previously unknown species of giant ground sloth. Wistar kept the taxonomical name *Megalonyx*, but added *Jeffersoni* to it, to honor the man who would soon become America's third president.

Paleontologists later determined that the 12-foot-long creature, which weighed a ton or more, browsed through the forests of what is now West Virginia more than 30,000 years ago. The West Virginia Legislature designated the giant ground sloth the official state fossil in March 2008.

and Jethro at Charleston's Municipal Auditorium, followed by a New Year's Day gig in Canton, Ohio.

Auburn University freshman Charles Carr, whose father, a Montgomery taxi company owner, was a friend of Williams's, was hired to chauffeur the country music star to his New Year's shows.

When poor weather and slow driving conditions set in, Carr and Williams tried to fly to Charleston from Knoxville, Tennessee, but their plane had to turn back due to dense fog in Charleston. Williams canceled the Charleston show and resumed his road trip, hoping to make it to Canton in time for a 2:00 p.m. performance the following day. Shortly before dawn, the two stopped at a Bluefield cafe, where Carr got a bite to eat, and Williams stretched his legs. Carr stopped at a diner south of Oak Hill to check on Williams, who had been sleeping in the back seat. When Carr moved the performer's hand, he felt an "unnatural" resistance, prompting him to head to the nearest hospital, which turned out to be Oak Hill General, where Williams was pronounced dead on arrival, the result of a massive heart attack.

A group of civic boosters and Williams's fans had planned to build a small museum in the vacant Pure Oil station in Oak Hill where Carr had reportedly stopped to seek directions to the emergency room a couple of blocks away. But in 2006 the owner of the station had the building torn down, and the museum plans went on indefinite hold. Each year hundreds of Hank Williams's fans retrace the path of the singer-songwriter's last ride, making stops in Oak Hill at the old hospital, now named Plateau Medical Center; Tryee Funeral Home, where Hank Senior was prepared for the ride back to 'Bama; and the Skyline Drive-In at nearby Hilltop, where Carr reportedly sought the whereabouts of the nearest hospital.

Signs along the stretch of Old US 19 passing through downtown Oak Hill designate the route as the Hank Williams Sr. Memorial Highway. A plaque memorializing Williams's Oak Hill death, embedded in a stone monument in front of the Herbert E. Jones Library, is the only

Last stop on the Hank Williams Highway is the old Oak Hill Hospital, now called the Plateau Medical Center.

other official acknowledgment of the country music legend having passed away while passing through the town. For more information, visit www.fayettecounty.com, or call (304) 465-5617.

Making Radio Waves

Princeton

The nation's first broadcast of a murder trial direct from the courtroom took place in 1931, when Bluefield's WHIS covered proceedings against Minnie Stull, a Mercer County woman accused of scalding her stepson to death.

The trial took place in Princeton's American Legion Building, across the street from the site of the new Mercer County Courthouse, still under construction at the time of the trial. Since there was no room for spectators in the temporary courtroom, the presiding judge suggested that the radio station set up loudspeakers to allow people gathered outside to hear the proceedings. The station owner received permission to take the suggestion a step further and broadcast the trial live, using several carbon microphones nestled in cotton-packed shoeboxes to reduce noise interference.

Stull was convicted of murder and given a death sentence, but her attorney successfully appealed the conviction on grounds that broadcasting the trial placed the proceedings in a "circus" atmosphere. A second trial was held in Greenbrier County, without radio coverage, where Stull was convicted for a second time but this time handed a life sentence.

Robert E. Lee's Ride

Rainelle

Camped atop Sewell Mountain near the Fayette–Greenbrier County line in the fall of 1861, Robert E. Lee took note of a handsome, high-spirited, four-year-old horse with a springy, fast-paced walk being ridden by a Confederate major from Charleston named Thomas Broun.

"He took a great fancy to it," Broun said in an 1886 *Richmond Dispatch* article. "He called it his colt, and said he would use it before the war was over." The horse, then named Jeff Davis, was bought by Broun from Captain James Johnston of Blue Sulphur Springs in Greenbrier County and later placed in the care of the Charleston man's brother, Captain Joseph Broun. After Union forces abandoned their position on a nearby slope with the arrival of winter, both Lee and Captain Broun were assigned to work on strengthening the coastal defenses in South Carolina. During a chance encounter between the senior and junior officer near Pocotaligo, South Carolina, in February 1862, Lee recognized Broun and his steed and enquired jokingly

Diamond in the Rough

What are the odds of having sixteen consecutive sons? Probably about the same as finding America's largest diamond in your backyard while pitching horseshoes. But both unlikely occurrences happened to Grover and Grace Jones of Peterstown in Monroe County.

The Joneses produced sixteen boys before their first and only daughter was born, a feat that earned the family a trip to the World's Fair in New York in 1940, where they met President Franklin D. Roosevelt and were interviewed on NBC Radio.

Celebrating the
PETERSTOWN, W. VA.
"Grover Jones Family Day"
New York World's Fair- Oct.3,1940

The Jones family of Peterstown produced sixteen consecutive sons and the nation's largest alluvial diamond. West Virginia Archives

Two years later, the huge West Virginia family would learn that they were part of an equally remarkable feat that began in April 1928. That was when Grover Jones, a schoolteacher, was pitching horseshoes with his twelve-year-old son, William "Punch" Jones, who discovered a clear, bluish piece of what he thought was quartz in the yard during the course of the game. Punch Jones placed the pretty rock in a cigar box he kept inside a toolshed and apparently didn't think a great deal more about it until 1942.

After reexamining the rock, which had apparently washed out of Rich Creek, a small stream running alongside the family's home, Punch Jones became convinced that it could be a diamond. He contacted Virginia Tech geology professor Roy Holden, who examined the stone and, to his surprise, determined that it was in fact a diamond—the largest ever found in North America at that time. The 34.48-carat gemstone measured ⅝ inch across, with a dozen natural diamond-shaped facets.

Punch Jones's luck ran out shortly after his find was verified. After enlisting in the Army, he was killed in action in 1945, as World War II was drawing to an end.

The Punch Jones Diamond was loaned to the Smithsonian Institution, where it remained until 1964, when it was placed in a safe deposit box in a bank in nearby Rich Creek, Virginia. When Grover Jones died in 1976, family members sold the diamond through Sotheby's auction house in New York to an agent representing an Asian lawyer for $74,250.

The only diamond ever found in West Virginia remains the largest alluvial, or stream-borne, diamond found in North America and is the third-largest diamond of any type found on the continent.

about the health of "his" colt. Broun offered to give the horse to the general, who immediately declined the offer. But he agreed to buy the mount if it performed suitably during a weeklong test ride.

Lee was pleased with the horse, and Broun offered to sell it to him at the $175 price his brother paid for the steed. Lee agreed but added $25 "to make up for the depreciation of our currency between September 1861 and February 1862," according to Broun. Lee renamed the horse Traveller. The gray steed was his constant

Gilligan's Heartland

After gaining fame as the clueless deckhand marooned on a desert island for ninety-eight episodes of *Gilligan's Island*, the actor Bob Denver drifted into the obscure southern West Virginia town of Princeton in 1995 and spent the rest of his life there.

Denver and his wife, Dreama, a native of the Princeton area, set up an FM station (WGAG, FM 93.1 "Little Buddy" Radio) in their downstairs game room, featuring an eclectic mix of oldies, blues, and rock through the decades. They also launched a Web site (www.bobdenver.com) to keep fans in touch with Denver's appearances, post trivia, and sell gift items. Both the radio station and the Web site are still up and running, though Denver died in 2005.

In West Virginia, the Denvers took part in numerous charity events, including hosting a "Two-Hour Cruise" down the Kanawha River aboard the sternwheeler *P. A. Denny* to raise funds for the Make-A-Wish Foundation.

Little Buddy Radio can be heard online at www.bobdenver.com.

companion throughout the duration of the war. After the war, Traveller accompanied Lee to his postwar job at Washington University in Lexington, Virginia, where souvenir hunters plucked hairs from his tail. During Lee's funeral in 1870, Traveller walked behind the caisson carrying the Confederate general's casket. He died the following year after developing tetanus.

A roadside marker along US 60 on Sewell Mountain points out the spot where Lee was camped when he first encountered Traveller.

Feudal Leader
Sarah Ann

In historic photographs, William Anderson "Devil Anse" Hatfield, the patriarch of one clan embroiled in America's best-known and bloodiest family feud, is often seen glaring stonily at the camera, a clutched weapon sometimes appearing beneath his bearded face.

These days, Devil Anse's stone-faced glare is made of Carrara marble and is part of a life-size statue that towers above other graves in the Hatfield Family Cemetery at the tiny coal-mining community of Sarah Ann, along Island Creek in Logan County. Two of Hatfield's sons commissioned the work following the clan leader's death from pneumonia in 1921, paying $3,500—a small fortune for the time—to have his likeness carved by Italian artisans, who based their work on photos supplied by the family.

The statue is mounted atop a 10-foot tiered pedestal, on which the names of the clan leader's wife, Levicy, and their thirteen children are listed.

Reached by a short dirt road off WV 44, the statue is listed on the National Register of Historic Places.

While more than a dozen people died during thirty years of feuding between the Hatfield and McCoy families, bitter feelings have long since died away. Starting in the 1990s, the two families began a tradition of holding joint family reunions in Matewan and Williamson, two Tug River towns along the Kentucky border where much of the

A statue of the Hatfield family patriarch "Devil Anse" Hatfield towers over the cemetery at Sarah Ann.

feuding took place. These days, the only struggle between the two families involves friendly competition during reunion events, including a half-marathon foot race and a tug-of-war across the Tug River.

To reach the Devil Anse Hatfield grave and statue from Logan, follow WV 44 south about 14 miles. Look for a Hatfield Cemetery sign on the right. Park at a small pull-off area near the sign and walk up a short but steep hill to the cemetery.

Carnival of Souls?
Spanishburg

The rusting hulk of a Ferris wheel, its base overgrown with weeds, rises eerily above the treetops in a patch of land along US 19 between Princeton and Spanishburg. Nearby, a corroded mechanical swing ride is perched near the bank of a pond, its rusting chains supporting a circle of decaying wooden seats.

Welcome to the former Lake Shawnee Amusement Park, a popular gathering place for coal-mining families across southern West Virginia from the 1920s to the 1960s. It is now better known in paranormal circles as a hot spot for lost souls who once lived on this stretch of floodplain along a bend of the Bluestone River.

Gaylord White, the current owner, worked at the park in its heyday in the 1950s and briefly reopened it after buying the land in the 1980s. He initially had plans of converting the tract into a residential development, but as he did some preliminary excavation work around prospective home sites, he began turning up a number of Native American artifacts and burial sites. In the 1980s archaeologists excavated an Indian village on the property that dated back to the 1500s. The village, which had been protected by a log palisade, was found to contain the graves of thirteen people, all but one of them young children. Also buried nearby are two children of the county's first European settler, Mitchell Clay, who settled the same stretch of the Bluestone in 1775. The Clay children were killed in a 1785 Shawnee raid. In the early 1950s a young girl died on the amusement park's

The former Lake Shawnee Amusement Park is now a
haunt for ghost hunters. Lawrence Pierce

swing ride, when a soft drink truck accidentally backed into the path
of the whirling swing seats.

Local stories of ghostly apparitions and the former amusement
park's eerie look have prompted a number of people to visit the site
long after its closing. Interest in the park peaked after the ABC Family
Network featured Lake Shawnee in a segment of its *Scariest Places on
Earth* series. White said that during the filming of the segment, a psy-
chic hired by the network to visit the park and report on its paranormal activity refused to stay, citing an overpowering spiritual presence.

White himself reports having first sensed, and later seen, the
ghostly presence of a girl in a pink dress with ruffled sleeves while

cutting brush on his tractor near the former amusement park. He said he has also occasionally heard people chanting, although no one could be seen at the time of the encounters.

"A lot of people have been touched by spirits here," White said in a 2007 newspaper interview. "I think the people who are able to see or feel them are blessed, for whatever reason. I always feel relaxed when I'm out here. . . . I'm at peace with all this. Maybe some day I'll figure it all out."

White, who lives on the property in a large mobile home and maintains a pay-to-fish lake there, asks that visitors get permission before touring the grounds on their own. He occasionally hosts night tours of the park and often opens the park for Halloween tours.

The ghostly ruins of the amusement park can be seen from the road near the junction of US 19 and WV 10, about 5 miles north of Princeton. If the pay lake is open, bring your imagination, along with your tackle, as the carnival grounds surround the lake. There is no listed telephone number for the pay lake or for White.

Two-State Tee Shot
Sprigg

Tug Valley Country Club's longest and most challenging hole may be its 425-yard, par-four 7 hole, but two other holes require golfers to hit the ball into another state before reaching the green.

Located near the Mingo County town of Sprigg, the 9-hole course is built along the banks of the Tug Fork River, which forms the West Virginia–Kentucky border. The course's 2 hole involves teeing up in West Virginia and putting out in Kentucky, while on the 6 hole, golfers drive from a tee in Kentucky to a green in West Virginia. A swinging, wood-decked cable suspension bridge carriers golfers and their carts across the border.

To reach the multistate golf course from Williamson, follow WV 49 south about 8 miles. Tug Valley Country Club, 282 Country Club Drive, Sprigg; (304) 235-2106.

Sin City
Thurmond

The world's longest-running poker game could have gone well beyond the fourteen-year mark had the Dunglen Hotel not burned to the ground in 1930.

The three-story, 120-room hotel was built in 1901 just across the New River from the coal and railroad town of Thurmond. It featured gambling ranging from roulette to poker, a bar that operated round-the-clock, a bank, big-city bands, a restaurant that featured fresh seafood brought by rail from Chesapeake Bay, a grocery store, and a rough-and-tumble "anything goes" atmosphere that may have had something to do with its final amenity—a mortuary.

Frequented by coal operators, politicians, and entrepreneurs of all stripes, the hotel, located deep in the New River Gorge, was a hideaway for the well-connected, virtually inaccessible by any means other than railcar. In the casino section of the hotel, fortunes traded hands routinely, and according to local legend, at least, a poker game that began sometime in 1916 didn't conclude until the July 22, 1930, fire that destroyed it.

To reach Thurmond from Oak Hill, follow US 19 south about 3 miles to Glen Jean, then turn left on Thurmond-McEndree Road. Follow Thurmond-McEndree Road about 6 miles to the New River, and cross the river on the combination rail trestle/car bridge to the Thurmond Visitor Center, managed by the National Park Service.

You Take Paradise . . .
Welch

Welch, the largest town in McDowell County and the seat of county government, may not have been paradise to the thousands of coal miners and their families who spent much of their leisure time strolling its crowded sidewalks in 1940, but it was certainly a popular destination. Crammed into a narrow valley of the Guyandotte River,

Détente, Y'All!

It took a plea for help from the Soviet Union for the tiny border town of Vulcan to get a fallen bridge connecting their community to the nearest highway replaced.

In 1977 a footbridge linking Vulcan to Kentucky's Route 194 washed away, leaving the thirty or forty families living on the West Virginia side of the Tug Fork River without a safe way to get in or out. After attempting unsuccessfully for months to get state or federal officials to show signs of interest in replacing the bridge, Vulcan resident John Robinette sought assistance from the Ford Motor Company. When that failed to produce results, he decided to try to shame government officials into action by seeking help from the Soviet Union. He sent a letter to the Soviet embassy in Washington, D.C., and a short while later, Iona Andronov, a correspondent for the *Literaturnaya Gazeta*, appeared in Vulcan to check out Robinette's complaints.

Robinette said the Soviet reporter told him that if the state and federal government failed to build a new bridge, the Soviet Union would. After the incident drew international attention, bids were accepted by the state's Division of Highways for a new span, and in 1980, a new one-lane-wide concrete vehicle bridge was completed at a cost of $1.14 million.

After the bridge was built, a movie deal was pitched based loosely on the Vulcan Bridge story. In it the Robinette character and a female Soviet journalist fall in love, get the bridge built, and live happily ever after together in Vulcan. So far, no studio has produced the concept.

Welch was a city of narrow, shop-lined streets and the center of commerce for the nearly 100,000 people who lived in McDowell County during the prewar coal boom.

As the industrial boom that accompanied the approach of World War II reached its peak, Welch was such a popular destination that traffic on its small grid of streets was perpetually jammed, and illegal parkers were making it impossible for fire trucks and ambulances to respond to emergencies. To ease congestion, the Welch City Council voted to put the idea of building a city-owned parking lot capable of holding 400 cars up to a popular vote. The measure passed by a margin of 881 to 113, and on September 1, 1941, the nation's first municipal parking garage opened to the public. The multilevel reinforced concrete building, which cost $108,000 to erect, turned a profit in its first year of operation. But after reaching a peak of about 105,000 people in the early 1950s, McDowell County's population steadily dropped. Today, only about 25,000 live in the county, after demand for coal plummeted, mechanization replaced many miners' jobs, and the area's deep mines ran out of recoverable coal. The parking building was renovated in 2005 and is still in use, but finding a good downtown parking space poses little challenge these days.

Stamping Out Hunger

Welch

On May 29, 1961, Henderson's Supermarket in Welch became the first grocery store in America to dispense food in exchange for a medium other than cash or checks.

As a busload of national press corps members looked on, Secretary of Agriculture Orville Freeman presented Chloe and Alderson Muncy of the McDowell County town of Paynesville with $95 worth of food stamps, which the couple promptly used to buy groceries at Henderson's to help feed their thirteen children. Their first food stamp purchase—a can of pork and beans—made them the first American family to make use of the new food voucher system.

President John F. Kennedy was moved by the poverty he encountered in Welch and other Appalachian towns while campaigning for the presidency. Upon taking office, he made the expansion of food distribution to the nation's low-income citizens his first executive order. The Muncys were soon joined by millions of other American families in putting the nutrition assistance program to use.

House of Fuels
Williamson

If the Tug Valley Chamber of Commerce Building should ever, God forbid, go up in flames, people in the Mingo County city of Williamson will be able to toast marshmallows for a month.

Smoking is strongly discouraged at the all-coal Tug Valley Chamber of Commerce Building.
Kenny Kemp

Blazing Her Own Trail

From the hills surrounding her childhood home along Twelvepole Creek near Wilsondale in Wayne County to dance poles in burlesque halls across the nation, Blaze Starr bumped and ground her way to the top in the world of exotic dancing.

Born Fannie Belle Fleming in 1932, the statuesque redhead adopted her showbiz moniker after taking up striptease following a move to Washington, D.C., at the age of sixteen. Famous for her onstage enthusiasm and disrobing with the assistance of a variety of props, ranging from a live panther to a sofa that produced simulated smoke, Starr became the burlesque queen of Baltimore and eventually the nation.

While dancing at a Bourbon Street nightclub in New Orleans in the late 1950s, she became involved in a long-term affair with then-governor Earl Long. That time of her life was featured in the 1989 movie *Blaze*, in which Paul Newman played Long and Lolita Davidovich portrayed Starr.

After hanging up her G-string in 1983, Starr took up gemology. In recent years she has sold her jewelry, marketed as Blaze Starr Gems, at a shopping mall in Eldersburg, Maryland, and online at www.blaze starrgems. According to her Web site, she recently moved back to her native West Virginia.

The chamber's office is located in the Coal House, a structure built in 1933 of 65 tons of high-quality coal blocks. The Coal House—which actually should be called the Coal Office, since it has never been used as a residence—was the idea of Norfolk & Western Railroad official O. W. Evans. Evans sought to promote Williamson's status as the town in the heart of an abundant coal region, which he dubbed the "Billion-Dollar Coal Field."

A coat of weatherproofing varnish is applied to the exterior of the building every other year to keep it shiny and dry. Inside, the structure's coal composition is not so noticeable, thanks to walnut paneling, wall-to-wall carpets, and central heat and air.

The Coal House is located on Second Avenue near the Mingo County Courthouse.

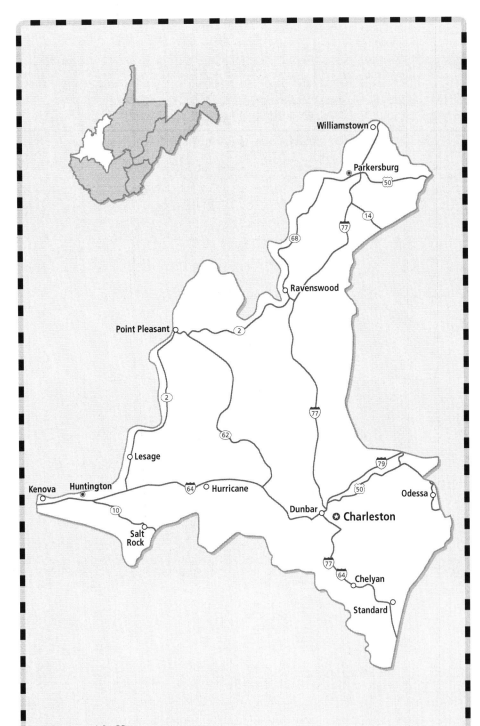

Metro Valley

2

Metro Valley

While it accounts for less than 10 percent of the state's land mass, the relatively flat area stretching between West Virginia's two largest cities—Charleston and Huntington—holds 30 percent of its population. So it goes without saying that a lot of characters have spent time here. They include Daniel Boone and George Washington, Billy Crystal and Soupy Sales, Charles Manson and Sara Jane Moore, Nick Nolte and Jennifer Garner, and Chief Cornstalk and Chuck Yeager.

Cole Younger and other members of the James Gang were reportedly responsible for Huntington's first bank robbery, while a being called Mothman allegedly terrorized the town of Point Pleasant, made the Silver Bridge collapse, and inspired Richard Gere to pursue a cinematic role that included a love interest with a Point Pleasant policewoman.

While it lacks a coastline, it is home to a Coast Guard station and one of the nation's largest and busiest ports. It is the birthplace of the Golden Delicious apple, the Big Boy hamburger, and Hillbilly Hotdogs. It is worth a visit.

★ ★

Burger Baron

Charleston

Atop a 30-foot pedestal at the corner of Patrick Street and Kanawha Boulevard, a huge fiberglass figure of a grinning, chubby youth clad in a red-and-white checked jumpsuit holds aloft a burger on a platter and gazes at a sweeping vista of Charleston's West Side. It's Big Boy, an American fast-food icon during the latter half of the twentieth century and the onetime mascot of a chain of more than 300 Big Boy restaurants in thirty-five states.

The Burger Boy Monument shows its buns at the site of the first Shoney's restaurant.

The Big Boy monument stands on the site of the first Shoney's restaurant, which began its career in 1947 as the Parkette Drive-In, founded by Charleston businessman Alex Schoenbaum. In 1951 Schoenbaum bought the rights to a new southeastern fast-food franchise called Burger Boy and two years later renamed the Parkette Drive-In "Shoney's," following an employee contest to find a new monicker for the restaurant.

The Shoney's Big Boy chain spread throughout the Southeast and Midwest and morphed from a burger stand into a sit-down, roadside coffeehouse featuring low-priced, down-home entrees and all-you-can-eat salad bars and breakfast bars.

Schoenbaum, a generous contributor to Charleston area charities, died in 1996. The site of the first Shoney's was cleared to make way for a new regional hospice headquarters. The Schoenbaum family reserved a small portion of the two-acre tract near the corner of Kanawha Boulevard East and Patrick Street to erect the monument to Shoney's fast-food empire.

Cult Connections
Charleston

While he will always be linked to the carnage he created in the Hollywood hills in 1969, the hills of West Virginia have more connections to cult killer Charles Manson and members of his family than state tourism officials probably care to remember.

Born in 1934 in Cincinnati, Manson moved to Charleston with his mother while a toddler. At the age of five, he was sent to live with his aunt and uncle in McMechen, a factory town near Wheeling, after his mother and an uncle were arrested and convicted of using a soda bottle to beat and rob a Charleston service station attendant. Manson returned to Charleston in 1942, following his mother's parole, but was soon sent to a reform school in Indiana. While living on Charleston's West Side, he frequented the same candy store that was also the childhood haunt of another state criminal luminary, Sara Jane

Youngest and Oldest

Getting elected governor as a Republican in an overwhelmingly Democratic state is no easy feat. Getting elected twice is even harder. But former West Virginia governor Cecil H. Underwood's service as the state's twenty-fifth and thirty-second chief executive had an even more unique distinction: Underwood was both the youngest and oldest governor in state history.

Underwood, then a high school biology teacher, began his political career at the age of twenty-two in 1944, when he was elected to the first of six terms in the state House of Delegates. The young Republican served as House minority leader during four of those terms and decided to take on Charleston mayor John Copenhaver in the 1956 gubernatorial primary. He won by 7,200 votes and went on to trounce Democratic U.S. Representative Robert Mollohan in the general election. After the election but before his inauguration, Underwood, then twenty-five years old, appeared as a guest contestant on the first-ever

Cecil Underwood was both the state's youngest and oldest governor. West Virginia Archives

episode of the new CBS game show *To Tell the Truth*, where his status as his state's youngest governor was featured. Since governors at that time were limited to one term in office, Underwood ran for the U.S. Senate after his four years in the governor's mansion were drawing to an

Underwood as a young man. West Virginia Archives

end. He lost to the incumbent Democrat, Jennings Randolph. Underwood later ran unsuccessfully for governor three times between 1964 and 1976, but in 1996 voters swept him into office again at the age of seventy-four. He was defeated in 2000 by Democratic Congressman Bob Wise.

During his terms in office, Underwood continued the process of desegregating West Virginia's schools, helped create a statewide system of mental health facilities, oversaw the last three executions in the state, and served as cochairman of the Appalachian Regional Commission.

Moore, who attempted to assassinate President Gerald Ford on September 22, 1975—seventeen days after Manson cult follower Lynette "Squeaky" Fromme made a similar bid.

After two stints in reform school and a series of incarcerations as a juvenile offender, he returned to Wheeling in 1954 at the age of nineteen, married his first wife the following year, and moved west.

In 1983, while serving time in a California prison following his conviction for masterminding the Tate–LaBianca murders, Manson wrote to the warden of the West Virginia Penitentiary in Moundsville, seeking to be transferred back to his childhood home.

"I was razed [sic] in McMechen & Wheeling," Manson wrote. "You may know some of my kin folks [sic]. God knows there have been enough of us in and out of your place. … Would you please accept me at your place? I got nine lifes, [sic] and I don't want out no more."

While Manson's request for a stay in a West Virginia prison was denied, two of his Tate–LaBianca codefendants, "Family" members Lynette Fromme and Susan Good, did serve time here, at the Alderson Federal Prison Camp for Women—the place where Sara Jane Moore served the first seven of her thirty-two years behind bars. Both Fromme and Moore briefly escaped from the facility, which became the focus of international attention in 2004, when Martha Stewart began serving a five-month stretch after lying to federal investigators about her sale of stock in an insider trading probe.

Hale of a Man
Charleston

It would take most people several lifetimes to accomplish as much—and have as much fun doing it—as John P. Hale did during his seventy-eight years, most of which were spent in and around Charleston.

The great-grandson of Mary Draper Ingles, an early settler of western Virginia who was abducted by Shawnee warriors and later escaped, Hale was a medical doctor and a graduate of the University of Pennsylvania who put his medical career on the back burner

John P. Hale built America's first brick street and founded the nation's first trust.
West Virginia Archives

in 1847 to manufacture salt from saline brines found in the Malden area just east of Charleston. Once that business was up and running, so was Hale, who went on a prolonged hiatus starting in 1851 to attend the World's Fair in London and tour continental Europe. Upon his return to Charleston, he created the first company to produce oil from cannel coal.

During the Civil War, Hale owned and operated the upper Kanawha River's first steam freighter, which he named *Here's Your Mule,* and after the war ended, brought to Charleston the state's first steam yacht, which he dubbed *The Pet.* After helping organize Charleston's first bank in 1868, he spent the 1870s founding or cofounding the city's first gas company, newspaper, theater, steam laundry, barrel factory, wholesale grocery, steam ferry service, and first steamboat line, with the vessels *Lame Duck* and *Wild Goose*.

In 1870 he introduced the nation's first brick street paving system to Charleston and, at his own expense, made Summers Street the first brick-paved street in America. The following year he began a term as mayor of Charleston and fronted the money needed to build the first Capitol building in Charleston, after playing a key role in the effort to move the seat of government from Wheeling. He then built Hale House, an upscale hotel to house legislators, and helped organize the county's saltmakers, of which he was the top producer, into the nation's first trust.

After writing several history books, Hale died in 1902 and was buried in the Old Circle section of Spring Hill Cemetery off Charleston's Farnsworth Drive, in a grave shaped like an Adena burial mound—his tribute to the industrious people who lived in the area a millennium before him.

Down and Out in South Hills

Charleston

More often associated with Beverly Hills than the green, rolling hills of West Virginia, actor Nick Nolte does have roots in the Mountain State.

Not long after marrying Rebecca Linger, the daughter of a Charleston physician, in 1984, Nolte moved to Charleston. Between acting gigs, he spent time hanging out on Hale Street at the Strand, a now-defunct pool hall, downscale restaurant, and card room, or going to sports bars with Charleston native and Los Angeles Rams linebacker Dennis Harrah.

The shopping cart–pushing homeless man he portrayed in the 1986 movie *Down and Out in Beverly Hills* was based on the Charleston street person Bill Dunn, known locally as "Aqualung" for his resemblance to the character on the Jethro Tull album of that name.

Nolte and Linger divorced in 1994. Their son, Brawley Nolte, is also

Dan'l Boone Kilt Some Time Here

While living in the Kanawha Valley in the 1780s and 1790s, the legendary frontiersman Daniel Boone blazed new trails as a politician.

Boone was one of the first men to represent the Kanawha Valley in the Virginia Assembly following the Revolutionary War. He was one of two Kanawha County men elected to the assembly in 1791, about three years after moving into the Charleston area from Point Pleasant, where he and his wife operated a small store, starting about 1786, after exploring and settling in the Kentucky country.

Boone, who worked mainly as a surveyor during his time in Kanawha County, lived in a two-room log cabin at the lower end of what is now the Kanawha City section of Charleston. Prior to his election, Boone was appointed a lieutenant colonel in the Virginia militia. He hunted when he found time, preferring the relatively wild country along the Gauley River to the more populated Kanawha Valley, and bought and sold horses and ginseng. By 1795 the Kanawha Valley had become too civilized for his liking, so Boone and a son moved west to the sparsely settled, Spanish-claimed Missouri country.

an actor, having appeared as Mel Gibson's son in *Ransom,* among other movies.

For a time during the 1980s, both Nolte and actress Jennifer Garner lived in Charleston's South Hills district. Garner, who moved to West Virginia from Texas at age four, was acting in community theater and George Washington High School productions during that time.

★ ★

Redneck Roots

Charleston

These days, the term *redneck* is associated with steel guitars, brassy attitudes, Jerry Springer, and change-resistant good ol' boys and girls from Yazoo City to Yakima. But the word's roots can be traced to the Mine Wars that raged through the southern coalfields of West Virginia in 1921, when an army of more than 5,000 coal miners

Striking miners formed the "Redneck Army" during the West Virginia Mine Wars. West Virginia Archives

marched from the Charleston area toward Logan to fight for the right to unionize.

As they marched toward the border of Boone and Logan counties, where they would encounter about 2,000 well-entrenched sheriff's deputies, hired thugs, and private detectives on Blair Mountain (see "Bombs Over . . . West Virginia?") many tied red bandanas around their necks so they could be easily identified by their allies.

The term was used by both friends and foes of the "Redneck Army," as the miners' force was known in many press accounts of the day.

Capital Punishment
Charleston

Once used by horse-drawn carriages carrying former governor William A. MacCorkle from Sunrise, his hilltop mansion, to the South Side Bridge and downtown Charleston, the Sunrise Carriage Trail now offers urban hikers a cool, leafy place in which to exercise and a viewpoint with a commanding panorama of West Virginia's capital city. But the ravine the trail crisscrosses has a violent past, which a marker along the path points out to those who take the time to read its inscription.

While digging up the right-of-way for the carriage path in 1905, workers came across the bodies of two unidentified women, one blonde and one brunette. MacCorkle had the remains reburied in a nearby grave that lay a few feet off the carriage path and set about learning what he could of who the women were and how they met their fate.

A former Union officer and city historian told MacCorkle that the two women were camp followers who were captured by Confederate troops encamped in Charleston in 1862. Charged with spying for the Union cause, the two women were tried and convicted during a hasty "drumhead" field court-martial, taken to the hollow in which their bodies were found, and executed by gunfire. Former Confederate

Grave consequences awaited suspected spies, who are buried along Charleston's Carriage Trail.

soldiers later challenged that story, saying that it was in fact a Union court-martial that led to the women's deaths.

The marker MacCorkle had placed at the site bears an inscription reading: "In the second year of the Civil War two women convicted as spies by drumhead court-martial were brought to this spot, shot and here buried. In 1905, when building this road to Sunrise, their remains were disinterred and reburied opposite this stone."

Since MacCorkle, a Charleston attorney who served as governor from 1893 to 1897, commissioned the grave marker to be carved and set in place in 1905, the identities of the two women have remained a mystery. To reach the Sunrise Carriage Trail from downtown Charleston, cross the South Side Bridge and make a sharp right turn at the south end of the bridge. Look for a small parking lot off Ferry Street on the left, only a few car lengths from the South Hills end of the bridge.

The 0.65-mile trail is open from dawn to dusk. For more information, e-mail carriagetrail@charter.net.

Down Under with Chuck Yeager
Charleston

Most people know Chuck Yeager as the irreverent, countrified test pilot and fighter ace who broke the sound barrier, was the basis for the book and movie *The Right Stuff,* and went on to pitch AC/Delco batteries on national television.

While Chuck Yeager broke the sound barrier in the Glamorous Glennis, he broke protocol in Charleston. West Virginia Archives

★ ★

But the over-fifty crowd in West Virginia's capital city best remembers Yeager as the aviator who caused their jaws to drop when he buzzed contestants in a hydroplane race at rooster-tail height just before flying under downtown Charleston's South Side Bridge.

On October 10, 1948, almost a year to the day after exceeding the speed of sound in a Bell XS-1 rocket plane, Yeager was in his home state to, among other things, perform a ceremonial flyover at a speedboat regatta sponsored by the *Charleston Gazette.* When the race emcee announced the imminent arrival of the sound barrier buster, boat race fans lining the banks of the Kanawha River and standing on the South Side Bridge looked upward.

But instead of making a showy, high-speed pass at a modest, FAA-approved elevation, Yeager, flying an F-80 Shooting Star, dropped to wavetop level after arcing past the state capitol building, undershot the bridge, performed a roll or two, then burned his way back to his base in California.

Viewers had to look down to take in most of the historic flight.

When Charleston's Yeager Airport was later named in honor of the famed aviator, Yeager seemed pleased but a little nonplussed: "Don't you have to be dead to have it named after you?," he asked a reporter.

A Little Gassy

Charleston

In 1815, when James Wilson drilled a well near what is now the intersection of Brooks Street and Kanawha Boulevard East in downtown Charleston, he was hoping to tap into a new source of salt brine for use in the Kanawha Valley's burgeoning salt industry. Instead, all he got was a lot of gas, which was quickly ignited by windblown sparks from a nearby campfire, lighting up the sky with bright flames. Wilson and his panicked crew didn't know what to do with the discovery, so they put out the fire and moved on, resuming their search for brine to support the area's fast-growing salt industry. It wasn't until 1841 that William Tompkins of Cedar Grove figured out a way to use natural gas to fuel brine evaporators, taking the place of charcoal and coal. His use of wooden pipes to bring natural gas to his salt furnace at Malden marked the nation's first application of natural gas in the manufacturing process. A historical marker at Brooks Street and Kanawha Boulevard East marks the site of Wilson's well.

Laddie Madonna?
Chelyan

Found by four teenage boys under a flat rock in a cave along a cliff overlooking the Kanawha River near Chelyan, the Kanawha Madonna has generated curiosity and controversy since its discovery in 1897.

Carved from a single block of honey locust, the Kanawha Madonna is a rough-carved, severely weathered 4-foot-tall statue of a human figure of indeterminate gender cradling a small four-legged animal to his or her chest. How it came to be named "Madonna" is as unclear as the facial features of the statue. Who carved it and what it is meant to represent also remain mysteries.

Radiocarbon testing in 1964 indicated that the wood used to carve the figure was about 350 years old, while a similar test forty years later showed the wood to be about 500 years old. Of course, the age of the wood may have little bearing on when the Kanawha Madonna was carved. Whether the statue was carved by a Native American or a latter-day hoaxer is also a matter of debate. The figure was found during an era in which hoaxes regarding fabricated Native American artifacts were not uncommon. But the Kanawha Madonna also bears similarities to wooden statues found at Native American sites in Kentucky and Georgia.

The Kanawha Madonna is housed in the West Virginia State Museum in Charleston.

From Taxes to Taxis

During his term as governor from 1953 to 1957, William C. Marland made headlines by attempting to take on the state's powerful mining industry and impose a tax on the extraction of coal. Marland, the son of a mine superintendent and a former miner himself, sought the coal severance tax to finance his plans to modernize the state's inadequate education and highway systems. But the scrappy young governor was better known for a situation that unfolded ten years after his battle with coal interests ended in defeat and his term in office drew to a close. It was then that the man who once steered West Virginia's ship of state was found to be recovering from a battle with alcoholism, making a living by steering the wheel of a Chicago taxicab.

William C. Marland launched a second career as a Chicago cab driver after leaving the West Virginia governor's mansion. West Virginia Archives

After graduating from West Virginia University law school and serving as a Navy officer in World War II, Marland's political star rose rapidly. Two years after beginning a stint as clerk for a federal judge in southern West Virginia, Marland was serving as West Virginia's attorney general, and by the end of his term he had become the Democratic nominee for governor. Thirty-four years old at the time of his inauguration, he was then West Virginia's youngest-ever governor.

In addition to butting heads with coal operators and their allies in the Legislature, Governor Marland was at odds with other southern governors in his support for the implementation of school desegregation, which took place during his term. During a 1954 meeting of the Southern Governors' Conference, Marland was the lone governor to voice support for federal desegregation policies. Term limit laws prevented Marland from seeking a second term as governor. The former governor made two unsuccessful attempts to win a U.S. Senate seat. After the losses, he resumed his law practice, and in 1959, he moved to Chicago to work in a bank.

Problems with alcohol that had begun in West Virginia intensified following Marland's move to Illinois. In an autobiographical piece he wrote for the Associated Press, Marland said that after arriving in Chicago, "my drinking had resolved itself into a twenty-four-hour-a-day proposition." He checked himself into the alcoholic ward of a mental hospital. After regaining sobriety, he took a job as a corporate attorney, but finding the high-pressure job harrowing, he sought an occupation in a "neutral zone" that would occupy his mind but not generate enough stress to make a return to drinking attractive.

Marland took what he thought would be a temporary job driving a white Ford sedan for Flash Taxi Company in Chicago. But he found himself enjoying the job enough that he remained a cab driver

(Continued)

until March 1965, when a *Chicago Sun Times* reporter followed up a tip that a former governor was working as a cab driver. The reporter conducted part of his interview with the former governor while he was enjoying an all-you-can-eat $1.25 chicken dinner in the basement cafe of a Chicago YMCA.

Marland was straightforward and matter-of-fact about his life after leaving the governor's mansion. When asked what brought about his turn of fate, he responded: "I got drunk." News stories about the long, strange trip his life had taken generated a number of job offers from West Virginia. He accepted an offer to work for the owner of two West Virginia horse tracks and returned to the state he once governed in April 1965, only to learn that he had developed pancreatic cancer. He died in November, eight months after leaving his job as a taxi driver.

Pillar of Tillers

Dunbar

In 1911, as Charleston photo studio owner Benjamin Franklin Gravely struggled with a hand-pushed plow to prepare his two-acre garden for planting, he had an idea: Why not use a motorcycle engine to power up the plow and save wear and tear on his back and legs?

The idea eventually struck a chord with millions of other backyard gardeners and lawn groomers.

Gravely's first garden tractor made use of an Indian brand motorcycle, a tractor wheel, and a series of belts. He made improvements on his original design and produced new versions of his tilling machine in his kitchen and basement.

Encouraged by friends and neighbors, he produced a half dozen tractors before he decided to manufacture them commercially at a former tire factory in nearby Dunbar in 1920. His Gravely Motor

Plows, which retailed for about $175 each, virtually sold themselves, and the Charleston man established sales outlets in Florida, California, France, and Switzerland within a few years after production began.

By 1926 Gravely was producing a two-wheeled garden tractor at the Dunbar factory. The tractors continued to sell well through the Great Depression, and by 1940 Gravely was ready to sell his stock and retire—perhaps to a place with no garden. He died in 1953.

The Dunbar factory closed in the 1960s, and Gravely's headquarters eventually moved to Wisconsin. West Virginia remains an occasional destination for annual "Mow-In" conventions of the Gravely Tractor Club of America, a collectors' club.

Portly Port
Huntington

The nation's largest inland port is not likely to attract a lot of stowaways—unless they are interested in running off to see exotic power plants or hoping to find themselves by traveling to far-off refineries. Coal and petroleum are the two biggest commodities passing through the Port of Huntington, which in 2005 was recognized by the Army Corps of Engineers as the nation's top river-based port, based on both tons loaded and trip ton miles, a calculation based on tonnage hauled and the mileage vessels travel to reach their destinations. Nearly eighty million tons of cargo, most of it coal, is shipped through the port annually, more than double the amount shipped through St. Louis, the No. 2 inland port.

Part of the reason for the port's No. 1 status has to do with the fact that its boundaries were dramatically increased in 2005. In 2004 the Port of Huntington was a 14-mile stretch of the Ohio River adjacent to West Virginia's second-largest city, Huntington. It shipped twenty-four million tons of freight that year. In 2005 the port area was expanded to include a whopping 100 miles of the Ohio River, plus the 90-mile navigable length of the Kanawha River and 9 miles of the Big Sandy River. The addition nearly quadrupled the number of

The nation's largest inland port stretches through nearly 200 miles of river.

tons of freight shipped from the Port of Huntington during the prior year. But the additional size of the port made things confusing. If you live in the Port of Huntington when your ship finally comes in, it will now be fifteen times harder to find where it's docked.

The Wild, Wild East

Huntington

After boosting $10,252 from a sleepy, small-town bank on September 15, 1875, members of the notorious James Gang made their getaway by galloping toward the border—the Kentucky border.

At least that's the most popular historical version of Huntington's first bank robbery. Since none of the James Gang's principals were killed or arrested in the heist, the composition of the holdup gang remains a matter of historical dispute.

Better known for stickups that took place in the Midwest and West, Jesse James and his crew, believed to include Cole Younger,

Thompson McDaniel, and Tom Webb (also known as Jack Keene and Tom Miller), are believed to have ventured just east of the Ohio River to hold up the Bank of Huntington in Huntington. After tethering their horses at Sanborn's blacksmith shop, one outlaw waited outside the bank while another entered a nearby store and stood lookout there. The remaining two outlaws entered the bank, brandished pistols, and demanded money from cashier Robert T. Oney. According to published reports of that time, the four bandits mounted their horses

Hillbilly Crystal?

Actor-comedian Billy Crystal's ties to West Virginia may not be the strongest in his life, but they are in the ballpark. Before the best-ever Oscar Awards host and the star of *When Harry Met Sally* became interested in show business, he was keenly interested in baseball.

While growing up in the Long Island town of Long Beach, New York, Crystal was captain of his high school's baseball team and its star second baseman. His skill on the diamond earned him a scholarship to Marshall University in Huntington. But shortly after checking into his freshman dorm, Crystal learned that Marshall's baseball program had been suspended, and he ended up never playing a game for the Thundering Herd.

In *700 Sundays*, his 2005 one-man, autobiographic Broadway show, Crystal jokingly lamented that he had earned a baseball scholarship to a college that did not have a baseball team, in a state where he recalled being the only Jew. After his baseball-free freshman year in West Virginia, Crystal transferred to New York University, where he studied film under Martin Scorsese, and his career took another path.

and trotted down Twelfth Street at a leisurely pace, then fired a fusil-lade of shots in the air when they reached the corner of Fifth Avenue before loping westward out of town.

That night, the crew ate dinner at the boardinghouse of Aunt Lizzie Christian in tiny Wayne before riding into Kentucky. Cabell County Sheriff D. I. Smith organized a posse and pursued the fugitives into the Bluegrass State. In Bell County, Kentucky, McDaniel and Webb were mistaken for horse thieves, and McDaniel was shot and fatally injured. Webb was later arrested in Tennessee, where he was found to be carrying $4,000 in cash from the robbery. James

The site of the 1875 James Gang holdup now sells software.

Shtick Figure

West Virginia was the launching pad for the self-proclaimed "Face That Launched 20,000 Pies." Soupy Sales (born Milton Supman) moved with his family to Huntington at the age of five. His stage name is an adapted form of a childhood nickname, Soup Bone, and there's probably a story there, too. It was in Huntington at the age of six that he earned laughs from a live audience for the first time while portraying Peter Rabbit in an elementary school play. He later said that response was like getting a message from above, pointing him on a path to a career in comedy.

After graduating high school in Huntington and serving a tour in the Navy in the South Pacific during the closing years of World War II, Sales returned to his hometown, where he earned a master's degree in journalism at Marshall University. While working on his advanced degree, he moonlighted as a deejay for a Huntington radio station but soon began his long career in television, starting by hosting a teen dance show for a station in Cincinnati.

After hosting his own network children's show, *Lunch with Soupy Sales*, he hosted his own *Soupy Sales Show*. From 1968 to 1975 he was a regular panelist on the game show *What's My Line?* and made several appearances as a guest on *Hollywood Squares*, a game show hosted by another television personality with Huntington roots, Peter Marshall. Marshall, whose given name is Ralph Pierre LaCock, wisely changed his last name to match that of the college in his West Virginia hometown.

and Younger apparently split the rest of the cash and continued their criminal careers.

Webb was returned to West Virginia, where he stood trial, and in December 1875 he was sentenced to twelve years in the state penitentiary at Moundsville. His sentence was commuted after serving ten years. Webb reportedly told authorities that the gang had come to West Virginia initially to rob a bank in Wheeling but decided to rob a B&O Railroad train instead, before thinking better of those plans and riding south to Charleston. After briefly scouting robbery prospects there, they went to Huntington and settled on the Bank of Huntington.

The bank building still stands in Huntington's historic Heritage Village and is located at Eleventh Street and Veterans Memorial Boulevard in downtown Huntington. It now houses a store that sells computer software.

A Museum at Its Zenith

Huntington

People whose interest in radio goes far beyond the morning zoo crew, shock jocks, and on-and-off switch can squelch out life's distractions for an hour or two by touring Huntington's Museum of Radio and Technology.

There's no static over the admission fees for visitors to the free museum, located in a ninety-year-old former elementary school building that is jammed with exhibits. They range from a 1920s radio shop with a working crystal set to a modern working amateur radio station with all the latest ham-friendly gadgetry. Radio buffs can triple their pleasure by visiting a mock salesroom chockfull of radios and early televisions from the 1940s and '50s; a 5,000-watt AM transmitter and studio complete with power supply components; and a display of military communications used by both allies and enemies.

The Museum of Radio and Technology is also the home of the West Virginia Broadcasting Hall of Fame, honoring radio and television personalities with West Virginia roots who have carved their own

Their master's voice is heard frequently at Huntington's
Museum of Radio and Technology.

niches in the airwaves. Inductees include Don Knotts, Grandpa Jones,
Bob Denver (see previous entry "Gilligan's Heartland"), and Soupy
Sales.

The museum, located at 1640 Florence Avenue in Huntington, is
open from 10:00 a.m. to 4:00 p.m. on Saturday and 1:00 to 4:00

p.m. on Sunday. From mid-April through October it is also open on Friday. Call (304) 525-8890 for more information.

Powerball Busted
Hurricane

Jack Whittaker was already riding high on Christmas Day of 2002 when he stopped at the C&L Super Serve in Hurricane to buy a $1 Powerball ticket that produced what was then the nation's biggest lottery jackpot of $315 million. A water-line contractor who was a millionaire several times over before entering the drawing, Whittaker initially seemed to relish his role as a colorful, happy-go-lucky bene-factor in a black cowboy hat. He elected to take a single payout of $170 million rather than the $315 million paid as an annuity, which left him with $114 million after taxes to begin doling out to churches, youth baseball leagues, senior citizen housing programs, and food pantries. He gave C&L Super Serve deli manager Brenda Higgin-botham, who served him bacon biscuits every morning, a new house and a new SUV and did the same for the clerk who sold him the win-ning ticket.

But it didn't take long for his luck to change. He had more than $500,000 stolen from a briefcase in his Lincoln Navigator while he partied in the Pink Pony, a Cross Lanes strip club. He was charged with groping a pair of female slot attendants at the nearby Tri-State Race Track and Gaming Center and charged with assaulting and threatening to kill the manager of Billy Sunday's, a St. Albans bar. He was arrested twice for drunk driving. His granddaughter was found dead of an apparent drug overdose, and his wife left him.

"I'm only going to be remembered as the lunatic who won the lot-tery," he said in an Associated Press interview. "I'm not proud of that. I wanted to be remembered as someone who helped a lot of people."

Out of His Gourd

Kenova

Ric Griffith's obsession began in 1978, when he carved four pumpkins into jack-o'-lanterns and placed them on the porch of his Victorian Kenova home in a subtle, artistic Halloween display—but decided he needed to do more. Each October that followed, his display got bigger and bigger. First, he attracted the attention of people across the river in Ohio, who phoned in house fire reports due to the glow from his illuminated pumpkin display. Then, after his Halloween display routinely included 3,000 or more jack-o'-lanterns and an army of volunteers to help scrape and carve them, Oprah and Ellen took notice and sent video crews to Kenova to report on the pumpkin-pumped pharmacist.

A Kenova pharmacist's 3,000-pumpkin Halloween obsession lands him on *Oprah*. Kenny Kemp

Griffith said his wife considers his over-the-top approach to Halloween to be symptomatic of obsessive-compulsive disorder. "But what does she know?" he said in a 2006 interview. "She's just a clinical psychologist."

Every eave, inch of porch space, windowsill, and stair step on his 1891 home is covered with jack-o'-lanterns. Others are displayed on multilevel, 20-foot-tall racks and on the larger limbs of the huge shade trees in his front yard. Many have lights that are wired into a computer, which in turn is connected to a classical music recording. The setup allows the jack-o'-lanterns to flicker and flash in time with pieces like Tchaikovsky's 1812 Overture.

The Halloween display draws more than 10,000 people each year to Griffith's 748 Beech Street home for only a few days of viewing, before the pharmacist recycles the jack-o'-lantern shells into livestock feed. Earlier, the seeds and pulp from the pumpkins are converted into pies, pumpkin butter, and snacks.

But when the pumpkins start to move beyond ripe, it's time to act. Otherwise, Griffith said, the nation's jack-o'-lantern capital "becomes the fruit-fly capital of the world."

Dog Diner Extraordinaire
Lesage

Drive down a straight stretch of WV 2 along the Ohio River near the Cabell County town of Lesage and you'll see an ancient school bus attached to a shack surrounded by beached motorboats, picnic tables, outhouses, and a half acre of preowned countrified schlock.

What appears to be a hastily arranged five-family roadside flea market is actually the world headquarters of Hillbilly Hotdogs, perhaps the best-known purveyor of West Virginia's favorite fast-food entree.

Owners Sonny and Sharie Knight, who have a flair for showmanship as well as wiener wizardry, have shaped their roadside stand into a tourist attraction, building a loyal local following from the Huntington area and drawing hotdog gourmets from across the region.

Since opening their original stand in Lesage in 1999, the Knights have opened Hillbilly Hotdog outlets in nearby Huntington and Lavalette.

While Hillbilly Hotdogs does produce a traditional West Virginia dog, it is better known for its exotic specialties, like the pepper-infused Rahall Dog, named after U.S. Representative Nick Rahall, a loyal customer who likes his hotdogs really, really hot; and the Junk-yard Dog, which includes all available condiments. Customers who can down a Homewrecker—a deep-fried, 1-pound, all-beef wiener smothered under another 2 pounds of condiments—in twelve minutes or less get a free T-shirt and directions to the nearest stomach pump. Most hotdog entrees cost $2 or less. The diner also sells burgers (watch out for the Double Wide), subs, and salads.

Slaw, chili, mustard, and onions are standard ingredients on a West by God Virginia hotdog.

Hillbilly Hotdogs' original diner is located at 6951 Ohio River Road (WV 2) in Lesage. It's open seven days a week, from 10:00 a.m. to 5:00 p.m. Call (304) 762-2458, or visit www.hillbillyhotdogs.com.

The Golden Bough
Odessa

Any way you slice it, it was Anderson Mullins's core belief that a "volunteer" apple tree he spotted growing in a pasture near an orchard in 1905 was something special. For the next nine years, he kept his eyes peeled on his Clay County farm to check the progress of the tree, which produced more fruit under adverse weather conditions than its pedigreed peers, tasted spicier, and remained crisp after months of storage.

Finally convinced that the tree could represent a strain of apple never seen elsewhere, he contacted the Stark Brothers mail-order seed company and sent officials there three apples from what he called the "Mullins Yellow Seedling" found growing on his property.

It was love at first bite for Paul and Lloyd Stark, who had never experienced such a spicy flavor before, especially from a yellow apple. Paul Stark set out almost immediately for the tiny Clay County community of Odessa, arriving on horseback after journeying by rail to the nearby town of Clendenin. According to the text of an old Starks company catalog, Paul Stark spotted the tree and noticed that its branches were bending to the ground under the weight of "a tremendous crop of great, glorious, glowing golden apples."

After buying the tree, all of its fruit for years to come, and a 900-square-foot chunk of Clay County soil surrounding it, Stark took cuttings of the tree for propagation and returned to his home office in Missouri. There, he came up with the name Golden Delicious, to pair it in sales with a recently developed red strain of apple that Stark Brothers had been marketing as simply Delicious.

Stark Brothers built a 30-foot-square cage of wire and wood around the tree to protect it from thieves and rigged it with an

It Ain't Hay

West Virginia's top cash crop is not the millions of bushels of apples and peaches it produces annually—although those using the state's No. 1 income-producing plant would likely savor them, along with chocolate, snack food, and assorted other munchies.

While apples and peaches bring in about $12 million a year, and much less tasty hay generates sales in the $60 million range, marijuana brings in an estimated $600 million or more annually to its West Virginia growers, according to the Department of Justice's Drug Intelligence Center.

Most of the state's pot production takes place in the southern half of the state, usually on property owned by absentee landowners, such as coal and timber companies. Helicopter-borne search-and-destroy operations targeting illegal pot patches are held annually, with varying results.

In the northeastern part of the state, the remnants of early-twentieth-century hemp fields still produce tons of low-grade pot along the South Branch of the Potomac River between Petersburg and Romney. There, hundreds of thousands of plants have been harvested and burned periodically by law enforcement personnel. It's not all that uncommon for area anglers and farmers to encounter strangers carrying garbage bags loaded with substances other than fish or corn along the stream banks and edges of fields.

The South Branch Valley's pot infestation can be traced to a Navy project dating to World War I, when several farms in the Circleville area were contracted to grow cannabis hemp for rope fibers. When the war ended, the hemp fields were plowed under and replanted with corn and other crops, but hardy hemp plants survived at the edges of fields, and floods carried their seed downstream.

In the early 1990s a record 1.1 million South Branch Valley hemp plants were slashed down and burned by state police and other law enforcement officials.

electric alarm to alert the Mullins family to any intruders. The tree survived for nearly fifty years.

The Golden Delicious apple is now the official state fruit of West Virginia. Each year the Clay County Golden Delicious Apple Festival salutes the popular fruit's West Virginia roots.

Fantasy Island
Parkersburg

After gunning down one of the nation's most popular Founding Fathers in a duel, where does a hotheaded former vice president go to escape notoriety and allegedly hatch a plot to establish an independent nation in Spanish-claimed territory in the American Southwest?

For Aaron Burr, Thomas Jefferson's former second-in-command, the answer was an island in the Ohio River in what is now Wood County, West Virginia. There, a wealthy Irish immigrant named Harman Blennerhassett had established a small plantation and built one of the grandest homes west of the Alleghenies.

Harman and Margaret Blennerhassett began building a frontier paradise on a 174-acre tract of land encompassing the north end of the island in 1798. By 1804—the year Burr shot and killed the Federalist leader Alexander Hamilton in a duel—the young couple had become the leading socialites of the Mid Ohio Valley. The Blennerhassetts entertained frequently and lavishly at their island mansion and likely attracted the attention of Burr, who was reportedly looking for financial assistance to carry out his nation-building scheme in the Southwest.

Burr spent considerable time on Blennerhassett Island in 1805, but despite its remote locale, word of his scheming eventually reached Washington. On November 27, 1806, President Jefferson issued an arrest warrant for Burr and his followers. The former vice president and his young, moneyed associate were arrested, jailed, and charged with treason but eventually acquitted due to a lack of evidence. Their reputations, however, were ruined. Burr moved to Europe, and

Blennerhassett and his wife moved to Mississippi and tried unsuccessfully to establish a cotton plantation before they, too, returned to Ireland.

The Blennerhassetts' mansion burned to the ground in 1811. Archaeologists unearthed its foundations in 1973, and during the 1980s, the state of West Virginia reconstructed the mansion on its original site. Blennerhassett Island is now a part of the West Virginia State Parks system. The island is open May through October and is accessible via a twenty-minute sternwheeler ride each way. Once on the island, visitors can tour the restored mansion, take a horse-drawn wagon ride around the former plantation, or rent fat-tired bikes to self-tour the 3-mile-long island's traffic-free dirt roads. Buy tickets for the boat ride to the island at Point Park in downtown Parkersburg. For information, call (304) 420-4800.

Aaron Burr's plot to carve a nation out of a chunk of the Southwest thickened on this Ohio River Island. Kenny Kemp

★ ★

Mothman Lives!

Point Pleasant

In 1966 reports of a creature with gray scaly skin, red eyes, a ban-shee-like scream, and a taste for dog flesh began to surface in and around the sleepy Ohio River town of Point Pleasant.

Since Ozzy Osbourne was eighteen and living in England at the time, emergency officials in Point Pleasant had to look elsewhere for the source of those mysterious reports. Numerous eyewitness accounts cited the West Virginia Ordnance Works, an abandoned explosives factory on the outskirts of town, as the place where encounters with the otherworldly creature began.

At the old Ordnance Works site, a number of domed bunkers origi-nally used to store munitions were leased to area chemical companies for storage of hazardous materials. Parts of the area remain an EPA

The stainless steel statue of Mothman, Point Pleasant's otherworldly being, shines on for visitors. Lawrence Pierce

Superfund toxic cleanup site. It was this milieu that spawned and nurtured the legendary Mothman.

In November 1966 two young couples were driving slowly through the grounds of the abandoned munitions plant when they approached an old generator building and spotted something moving toward a doorway.

"It was shaped like a man, but bigger—maybe 6½ or 7 feet tall. And it had big wings folded behind its back," one of the women in the car told sheriff's deputies. "But it was those eyes that got us. It had two big eyes like automobile reflectors."

When the two couples sped away from the site, the creature reportedly ran after their car, catching up to them as they approached a small hill. As their car crested the hill, the pursuing being began to fly, matching the vehicle's pace at speeds up to 100 miles per hour. As the car approached the city limits and the comparatively bright lights of Point Pleasant, the beast broke off the chase.

Scores of similar sightings took place in the weeks and months to follow, along with many cases in which electronic devices such as radios, televisions, and telephones were reported to have malfunctioned, apparently in connection with the creature's presence.

While the flying beast was initially called a giant bird by those who encountered it, the creature picked up a new and enduring name after the Associated Press news service picked up a story about it from the *Point Pleasant Register.* An AP wire editor dubbed the creature "Mothman," and its legend spread far beyond the borders of West Virginia.

The New York paranormal investigator and author John Keel connected a series of Mothman sightings, UFO appearances, and the tragic 1967 collapse of the Silver Bridge carrying traffic across the Ohio River between Point Pleasant and Gallipolis, Ohio, in which forty-six people died. His 1975 book *The Mothman Prophecies* formed the foundation for the 2002 movie of the same name, which starred Richard Gere.

Dueling: Banjos Only!

West Virginia law makes it a point of honor to take a dim view of participating in political hardball's hardest game: dueling. Jail terms of up to six months and fines of $100 can be levied for those found guilty of "taunting for nonparticipation in a duel." A related law disqualifies West Virginia citizens from holding office if they send or accept the challenge of a duel or act as a duelist's second.

Mothman sightings continue in the Point Pleasant area, but not with the same frequency in which they were reported in 1966 and 1967. A downtown Point Pleasant storefront houses the Mothman Museum (411 Main Street). In addition to displaying artifacts commemorating the life and times of the winged beast, the museum hosts bus tours of the old ordnance plant. A life-size stainless steel statue of Mothman, complete with glowing red eyes, adorns a traffic island in Point Pleasant, which hosts a Mothman Festival each September. For more information on Mothman activities in Point Pleasant, visit www.mothmanmuseum.com or its affiliated site, www.mothmanlives.com.

Heavyweight Horse
Point Pleasant

Decked out in a halter—the horse kind—and looking like Mr. Ed on steroids and mood elevators, General, the world's largest stuffed horse, takes up a good part of a display area at the West Virginia State Farm Museum near Point Pleasant.

While among the living, General, once owned by John Greene of Milton, was tall enough to play in the NBA and weighed more than the entire offensive line of, say, the Indianapolis Colts. The Belgian draft horse was 6 feet, 6 inches tall and weighed 2,850 pounds. He was the second-largest representative of his breed, in terms of both height and weight, and the third-largest horse that ever lived.

It cost $10,000 to have General stuffed and ready for permanent display at the museum, along with his pulling gear and a wagon he towed at draft horse shows. The fifty-five-acre West Virginia State Farm Museum showcases the state's rural life, with exhibits on livestock, farm machinery, the pioneer era, and farm towns. Located 5 miles north of Point Pleasant at 1458 Fairground Road, it's open April 1 through November 15 on all days but Monday and major holidays. For more information, call (304) 675-5737, or visit www.wvfarm museum.org.

The world's largest stuffed horse pulls his own weight while on display at the West Virginia State Farm Museum.

Art by the Mile
Point Pleasant

When it comes to art appreciation in the river town of Point Pleasant, there's no sitting on the wall—because if you're sitting on the wall, you're making it difficult for anyone to see the art.

The town's massive floodwall, a 15-foot-high concrete slab that keeps the Ohio and Kanawha rivers at bay during times of high water, is slowly and steadily being converted into an illustrated history of Point Pleasant by the muralist Robert Dafford.

Since 2006 Dafford and his associates have been painting scenes from the era of Lord Dunmore's War, a campaign launched in 1774 by Virginia colonists to protect settlers from attack as they moved into land also claimed by the Shawnee, Mingo, and other Native American tribes. The first 300-foot-long section of the floodwall is devoted to a colorful, realistic representation of the Battle of Point Pleasant, an engagement between about 1,200 Shawnee led by Chief Cornstalk and a like number of militiamen led by Colonel Andrew Lewis.

Dafford, a native of Louisiana, read numerous historic accounts of the battle, then consulted with historians and colonial and Native American reenactors in West Virginia, before planning his mural panels. Next, he used authentically costumed reenactors as models and took thousands of digital photos of them as he directed battle and encampment scenes in the woods around Point Pleasant.

Cornstalk and his warriors attacked Lewis and his militiamen early on the morning of October 10, 1774, but following a daylong, often hand-to-hand struggle, the Virginians prevailed, forcing the Shawnee chief to sign a treaty. Three years after surrendering to the colonists, Cornstalk was murdered by vengeful settlers at Fort Randolph, a Revolutionary outpost near present-day Point Pleasant.

A ½ mile of mural art is planned for the floodwall, with future panels to include scenes of Shawnee village life and the story of Mad Anne Bailey, who became a frontier scout after losing her husband in the Battle of Point Pleasant.

Point Pleasant's floodwall keeps the town dry and in touch with its roots.

More information on Dafford's work and several of his panels can be seen at Main Street Point Pleasant's Web site at www.point pleasantwv.org. The section of floodwall bearing the murals surrounds downtown Point Pleasant fronting the Ohio River and Tu-Endie-Wei State Park at the Kanawha River's confluence with the Ohio.

Chiseled Figures
Salt Rock

It took a lot of dedication, skill, and upper body strength to create enduring works of art in West Virginia during the centuries before European settlers began streaming westward across the Alleghenies.

West Virginia's oldest outdoor art includes images of birds, snakes, turtles, and people carved in stone. Kenny Kemp

Twenty-seven Native American petroglyph sites have been recorded at locations across the state, providing clues about the lives and belief systems of those who lived here before history was recorded. Petroglyph artists used stone tools, keen imaginations, and buckets of sweat to chisel the grooved outlines of ghostly human images, intriguing geometric designs, and stylized likenesses of wildlife appearing on the petroglyph rock faces.

The largest of the state's petroglyph sites is found between the towns of Salt Rock and West Hamlin on a narrow strip of land between a busy railroad track and the slow-moving waters of the Guyandotte River. The Salt Rock Petroglyph, first recorded in an 1848 survey by the Smithsonian Institution, includes a human figure, or anthropomorph, with an eerie facial expression that looks a lot like that of the anguished soul in Edvard Munch's famous paint-ing *The Scream.* Images of birds, turtles, and serpents, as well as a slightly larger-than-life human, can also be seen at the Salt Rock site. Although the Salt Rock site is located along a narrow, publicly owned dirt road, there are no signs marking its location and no parking facilities.

Unfortunately, acid rain and natural erosion have faded carvings at several sites almost into oblivion, and there has been little demon-strated interest in spending the money needed to preserve and pro-tect the state's best petroglyph sites.

Tunnel Vision
Standard

Back in 1987, when an upgrade of the West Virginia Turnpike (signed as I-77 for its entire length, I-64 from Charleston to just south of Beckley) required digging a 370-foot-deep trench through the moun-tain separating the Paint Creek and Cabin Creek watersheds, Major General Allen B. Tackett began developing an acute case of tunnel vision.

The massive cut, which involved moving 10 million cubic yards of earth, bypassed the turnpike's Memorial Tunnel—the first in the nation to make use of a television traffic monitoring system when it opened in 1954. After resting in peace for a few years after its closure, the tunnel was used occasionally from 1993 to 1995 by the Federal Highway Administration as a site to test tunnel ventilation systems designed to minimize fire risks. Information produced by the testing was incorporated in planning Boston's Central Artery/Tunnel project, better known as the Big Dig.

With the tunnel's fire-testing days over, Tackett, West Virginia's adjutant general, saw an opportunity to expand the tunnel's useful-ness by using it as a training center for a variety of military and civilian emergency response scenarios. The Department of Defense signed off on Tackett's plan and in 2000 began modifying the tunnel to build a

Getting hosed after a hazardous materials response drill is part of the Memorial Tunnel's training routine. Lawrence Pierce

number of training sets. They include a New York City subway station equipped with real subway cars, Broadway show posters, and graffiti; a mobile home methamphetamine lab; a collapsed parking building for extrication training; and a highway accident/incident scene.

Military operatives and civilian emergency responders from around the world have trained at the tunnel, which is now managed by the West Virginia National Guard as a component of the Joint Interagency Training and Education Center. The southbound entrance of the tunnel, over which a huge American flag is draped, can be glimpsed by turnpike users traveling between the Sharon and Morton service plaza exits, about 30 miles south of Charleston.

Island Warfare

Since West Virginia lacks a seacoast, it is not often associated with U.S. Navy vessels, let alone naval vessels used to fire on an enemy cavalry and infantry troops. But on July 19, 1863, a stretch of the Ohio River controlled by the newly formed state of West Virginia was the site of a naval operation that disrupted the retreat of a force of nearly 3,000 Confederate troops led by General John Hunt Morgan.

After raiding a series of towns across Ohio and Indiana, Morgan and his men, along with a wagon train of loot seized in the raids, left the Ohio shore of the Ohio River, crossed to Buffington Island, which lies in West Virginia waters, and attempted to cross a ford leading to the West Virginia mainland.

A force of Union infantry and cavalry troops was in hot pursuit of Morgan's force and began to overtake it just as the crossing was being attempted.

As daylight broke, sailors aboard the USS *Moose*, one of several federal gunboats dispatched to intercept the Confederates, heard gunfire as they approached Buffington Island. As the morning fog lifted, southern troops could be seen swarming toward the West Virginia shore. The *Moose* opened fire with its battery of 24-pound artillery pieces, killing nine Confederates, halting the rebel retreat, and forcing the raiders to abandon two cannons and a number of loot-laden wagons.

The *Moose*, joined by a hastily armed Union steamer, continued to fire on the Confederates as they attempted to cross at other sites. The naval action helped shorebound Union troops contain and capture elements of the rebel force, which surrendered a few days later near New Lisbon, Ohio.

One sailor on the *Moose* was struck on the wrist, and a deckhand on the other federal vessel suffered a buttock wound from small arms fire from the Confederates.

Islands in the Stream

Williamstown

Those interested in exploring nature on a remote chain of islands without leaving the state of West Virginia or taking illegal drugs should begin their trip with a stop in Williamstown.

Williamstown is the home of the Ohio River Islands National Wildlife Refuge's headquarters, where visitors can learn about the bird, fish, plant, and animal life found on and around the twenty-two islands managed by the refuge. Perhaps the longest and narrowest refuge in the East, Ohio River Islands National Wildlife Refuge

No boat is needed to reach Middle Island in the Ohio River Islands National Wildlife Refuge.

stretches nearly 400 miles, encompassing 3,354 acres of islands and small sections of shoreline. Most of the refuge lies in West Virginia, but several Kentucky and Pennsylvania islands are also within the refuge's boundaries.

The refuge was established in 1990 to save a rapidly dwindling amount of mature bottomland hardwood forest, as well as to preserve islands threatened by sand and gravel mining. The islands and their surrounding waters provide key habitat for such waterfowl as great blue herons, which nest on several of the islands, along with eighty other bird species. Bald eagles and ospreys feed on fish caught in the refuge's waters, where twenty species of freshwater mussels, including two that are endangered, are also known to live.

While all the refuge's islands are open to the public, only one—Middle Island at St. Marys—is connected by a bridge to the mainland. Hiking trails, an interpretive drive, and a wildlife viewing blind are available on 235-acre Middle Island, the largest island in the refuge. A new refuge visitor center opened at Williamstown in 2008, offering a number of exhibits on the islands' wildlife, plant life, and human history. A 1,200-gallon aquarium contains a sampling of live Ohio River fish. The visitor center is open from 8:00 a.m. to 4:30 p.m. Monday through Saturday, April through November, and from 8:00 a.m. to 4:30 p.m. Monday through Friday, December through March. To reach the visitor center, take Exit 185 off I-77, then follow WV 14 1.3 miles before turning right on Waverly Road/West Fourth Street. Continue 1.9 miles on Waverly Road to arrive at the center.

For additional information, call (304) 375-2923, or visit www.fws .gov/northeast/ohioriverislands.

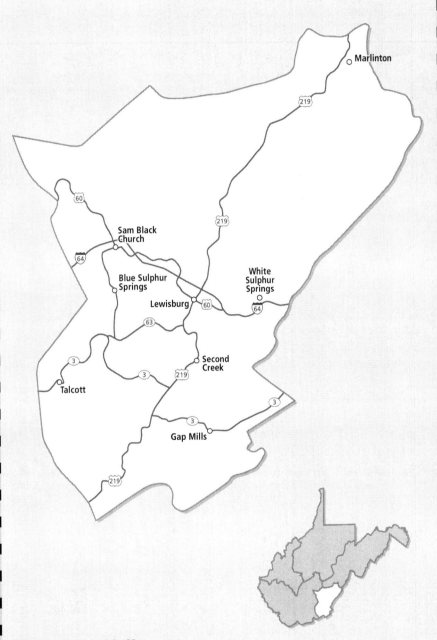

Marlinton

219

60

Sam Black
Church

64

Blue Sulphur
Springs

White
Sulphur
Springs

Lewisburg

60

64

63

3

Second
Creek

3

219

3

Talcott

219

3

Gap Mills

219

Greenbrier Valley

3

Greenbrier Valley

*A*fter its wider stretches were settled and farmed by colonists in the mid-1700s, the Greenbrier River Valley soon developed a reputation as a heat-beating getaway for coastal Virginia's planters and merchants, who apparently had a liking for water that smells like rotten eggs.

Resorts were developed at Blue Sulphur, Red Sulphur, Salt Sulphur, and White Sulphur Springs, giving the Tidewater gentry the chance to cure a variety of ailments in the stinky water and spend time kicking back in the shade with their well-to-do friends.

The area remains a blend of farm country, resort property, vacation homes, and old traditions, but with a new focus on art and fine dining. The Greenbrier at White Sulphur Springs is the last and the grandest of the valley's mineral water spas. It has hosted twenty-six presidents over the years and built a secret underground bunker to house and provide assembly halls for all members of Congress in the event of nuclear attack.

But one doesn't have to be rich or powerful to enjoy the treasures of this region. Lewisburg has its own Carnegie Hall, built by the same industrialist/philanthropist who built the one in Manhattan, which offers a wide variety of free or affordable concerts, exhibits, and clinics. Hiking and biking along the 78-mile Greenbrier River Trail is free, and inner-tube or canoe floats down the scenic river are cheap.

If you hanker for spring water that smells like rotten eggs but can't afford a stay at The Greenbrier, you can visit one of the valley's abandoned mineral spa sites and get stinking sober drinking your fill for free.

Pasture-ized Water
Blue Sulphur Springs

What's a Greek temple doing in the middle of a cow pasture along a narrow country road north of Alderson in rural Greenbrier County?

The weathered pavilion supported by a dozen Doric columns is all that remains of the Blue Sulphur Springs resort, a health spa and summer getaway that flourished in the 1840s, drawing visitors ranging from Robert E. Lee and Andrew Jackson to Henry Clay and Napoleon's kid brother, Jérôme Bonaparte. Today, the open-sided pavilion shelters the spa's original marble fountain from which clear "healing waters" with a strong aroma of sulfur constantly flows.

Built along Kitchen Creek in 1834 by George Washington Buster, the spa once included a three-story hotel with rooms for 200 guests, twenty cottages, and bathhouses for those either taking the waters or sampling the nation's first commercial mud baths.

While the resort drew the high and mighty of the era, it also had its critics, including William Burke, a travel writer of his day who wasn't afraid to call it as he saw it in a guidebook to mineral springs of Virginia: "Never have we seen bad taste more unfortunately illustrated than here," he wrote. "It seems as if the designer had his brain obfuscated by mint-julep."

Whether or not George Washington Buster had dependency issues with mint juleps is not known, but he did run into financial difficulties in the 1850s, when he had to compete for guests with the newly built resort at nearby White Sulphur Springs. In 1859 he sold the resort to a Baptist group that used the resort as a campus for the newly formed Allegheny College. The college had an inauspicious start. Its main dormitory, the former hotel building, burned to the ground in 1860, and the Civil War broke out the following year.

Both Union and Confederate troops used the old spa as a bivouac site. Despite Buster's claims that the spa water was an effective treatment for cholera, typhoid, diphtheria, dysentery, and various kidney and bladder maladies, eighty-nine Confederate troops from Georgia

A Greek temple in a cow pasture marks the site of the former Blue Sulphur Springs resort.

who camped at Blue Sulphur during the winter of 1861–1862 died of disease. In 1864 Union troops burned all the spa's remaining buildings except for the main pavilion, which is now listed on the National Register of Historic Places. You can still see the pavilion and take the waters from its fountain by traveling State Secondary Route 25, the Smoot–Sam Black Church Road, off the Dawson exit of I-64. But if you hike across the pasture to the pavilion, watch your step: In summer, there's a red alert in effect for cowpies.

Towering View

Gap Mills

Anchored to a large, slanted rock outcrop clinging to the 3,200-foot summit of Peters Mountain in the Jefferson National Forest, Hanging Rock Tower is not really a tower at all. The rock formation puts the cab of the lookout well above the tree line, negating the need for the customary long-legged understructure used by most fire lookouts.

In 1972 airplane-borne fire spotters replaced the seasonal fire observers at Hanging Rock, and the lookout station began to fall into disrepair. Members of the Charleston-based Handlan Chapter of the Brooks Bird Club and local hawk watchers on both sides of the Virginia–West Virginia border began to use the lookout as a sheltered vantage point for conducting hawk and eagle counts during annual raptor migrations. In 1984 the birders rebuilt the lookout, carrying lumber by hand along the 1-mile trail leading to the tower from Waiteville Road. The tower was burned down by vandals in 1996 but rebuilt the following year in a joint effort between the U.S. Forest Service and bird-watcher volunteers.

Since then thousands of birders and curious visitors from around the world have made the hike to what is now the Hanging Rock Raptor Observatory to take in the spectacular 360-degree view, which in the fall often includes an astonishing number of southbound hawks, eagles, ospreys, and falcons. Records of daily migration counts have been taken since 1974, when the biggest single-day tally for raptors took place on September 20, with 2,684 broad-winged hawks counted soaring past Hanging Rock.

To visit the tower from Gap Mills, follow Zenith Road west about 4 miles and then turn left on Limestone Hill Road and follow it to the top of the hill. Turn right at the top of the hill into a small parking lot, park, and follow Allegheny Trail south almost 1 mile to the Hanging Rock Tower spur trail. For updates on bird counts, photos of birds and bird watchers, and more information, visit www.hangingrocktower.org.

Carnegie Holler

Lewisburg

How do you get to Carnegie Hall?

In West Virginia you can either practice, practice, practice, or you can drive to Lewisburg, turn down Church Street, and look for a

New York's Carnegie Hall is not the only one built by the industrialist Andrew Carnegie.

stately Georgian Revival building with a portico framed by huge Ionic columns.

Lewisburg's Carnegie Hall was built by the steel baron Andrew Carnegie in 1902, twelve years after the first music hall bearing his name opened for concerts in midtown Manhattan. Lewisburg resident James Laing, who grew up in the same town in Scotland as Carnegie, asked the industrialist for help in replacing a classroom building that had been destroyed by fire at the Greenbrier College for Women. Carnegie donated the money needed to erect the building, which housed the women's school and later was the home of a mental health center for youth. A civic group rescued the building from possible razing and in 1983 converted it into a regional venue for artistic performances and exhibits. Performers appearing at the Lewisburg Carnegie Hall have included violinist Isaac Stern, bluegrass impresario Ralph Stanley, the Vienna Boys Choir, Arlo Guthrie, Harry Belafonte, and Wynton Marsalis.

Carnegie Hall West Virginia is located at 105 Church Street in Lewisburg. For information, call (304) 645-7917, or visit www.carnegiehallwv.com.

Cave Kid
Lewisburg

According to legend, Bat Boy, the winged, sight-impaired, sharp-fanged cave dweller who rose to fame from the pages of the supermarket checkout line tabloid *Weekly World News* in July 1992, was discovered in Lewisburg's Lost World Caverns by a biologist named Dr. Ron Dillon.

Since then, according to the tabloid, the 2-foot-tall, 20-pound creature has, among other things, eluded FBI agents attempting to apprehend him in his home cave, stolen a car, and served with the U.S. Marines in Afghanistan. Most recently, according to the highly impeachable source, Bat Boy endorsed the candidacy of Barack Obama in order to deliver him the "mutant vote," then crashed the new president's inaugural ball. The Bat Boy legend was the basis of the 1997 off-Broadway production *Bat Boy: The Musical.*

You can try to catch a glimpse of the winged wonder by touring Lost World Caverns, which, unlike its most famous resident, is unassailably real. It is also open to the public daily, except on major holidays. Even if you don't spot Bat Boy on Lost World's ½-mile self-guided tour, you will encounter a measure of otherworldly beauty in the cave's 150-foot-tall main room, which is loaded with stalactites, stalagmites, and flowstone features.

Among the larger features is the War Club, a 28-foot-tall stalagmite upon which Parkersburg caver Bob Adis sat his way to a place of honor in the *Guinness Book of World Records* in 1971. After rigging a small wooden platform to the top of the War Club with ropes, Adis remained on the 500,000-year-old underground pillar for fifteen days, twenty-three hours, and twenty-two minutes—without once seeing Bat Boy or his parents.

Tours of Lost World Caverns cost $10 for adults and $6 for kids ages six to twelve. Take the Lewisburg exit off I-64 and travel south on US 219 into Lewisburg before turning right on Washington Street, right again on Court Street, and following the signs to the Lost World parking lot and tour center. Call (304) 645-6677, or visit www .lostworld.com.

Rebels without a Name

Lewisburg

The men buried in the state's largest Confederate cemetery aren't forgotten, but since the time they fell in battle, they've never really been known.

The carefully tended, wrought-iron fenced cemetery found at the end of a grassy walkway off McElhenny Street in downtown Lewisburg

A mass grave in Lewisburg holds the remains of ninety-five unidentified Confederate soldiers. Kenny Kemp

contains a cross-shaped mass grave holding the remains of ninety-five unidentified southern soldiers. Most of them died within a few hundred yards of their final resting place, during the May 23, 1862, Battle of Lewisburg. The rest of the unknowns died during the November 6, 1863, Battle of Droop Mountain, about 20 miles to the east.

The earthen mound that marks their resting place measures 80 feet long and 35 feet wide and is the only remaining physical reminder of the Battle of Lewisburg, during which 1,200 Union troops under Colonel George Crook fought off an attack by a larger Confederate force, then pushed the southern force out of the Greenbrier Valley. Eighty Confederate soldiers died in the fighting, while the Union dead numbered thirteen. A part of the federal line of battle ran directly through the site of the Confederate cemetery.

Each May Union and Confederate reenactors restage the Battle of Lewisburg. For details on upcoming reenactments and photos of the Lewisburg Confederate Cemetery, visit www.battleoflewisburg.org, or send e-mail to info@battleoflewisburg.org.

The Spirit of the Law
Sam Black Church

The spirit of Zona Heaster Shue may be the only ghost to earn her own highway marker. Hers is found along US 60 near its intersection with I-64 in the sleepy Greenbrier County community of Sam Black Church. It was there, in 1897, that she was murdered—and according to legend, later appeared in her mother's home to identify her killer and ask for justice.

Zona Heaster had only recently been married to Edward "Trout" Shue, a little-known newcomer to the area, when Shue appeared at his mother-in-law's home, carrying the body of his bride. Shue insisted that his newlywed wife died of natural causes, and a coroner's examination concluded that she had died from complications of childbirth—even though Zona had told no one in her family that she was pregnant.

Mary Heaster, Zona's mother, was suspicious of Shue's story and discounted the coroner's report. Not long after her daughter's body was laid to rest in a nearby cemetery, she reported being visited four times by Zona Heaster Shue's spirit, who told her that her husband

Roadkill Cook-off

When people in the Pocahontas County town of Marlinton talk about meat on the grill, they may be referring to a radiator grill rather than the business end of a barbecue.

Each October Marlinton hosts the annual Roadkill Cook-off, a festival that celebrates a state law passed in 1998 allowing West Virginians to keep and consume game animals bagged by bumpers. The contest features cooks from across the state preparing recycled game entrees ranging from Deer Smear and Thumper Meets Bumper to Tire Tread Tortillas and One-Ton Wonton on camp stoves and in Dutch ovens.

While contest rules require contestants to scrape any "gravel, tar, or rubber" off their entries, the food is usually wild game fare harvested through more conventional means. Taking to heart the cook-off's motto of "You Kill It, We Grill It," cook-off rules allow the use of any critter that is commonly recycled after being tenderized by tires. So in addition to bear, deer, turkey, and squirrels, entrees often include possum, groundhog, rabbits, turtles, and frogs.

Reaching Marlinton by road from any direction involves a long drive through the Monongahela National Forest, giving cook-off attendees the chance to bring food from the "take-out" menu.

For details on the next Roadkill Cook-off, visit the Pocahontas County Chamber of Commerce Web site at pccocwv.com.

had murdered her in a fit of rage over her forgetting to include fruit with his lunch.

Mrs. Heaster, who was well respected in the Sam Black area, began urging the county's prosecuting attorney to look into Shue's role in her daughter's death. After several months of cajoling, he ordered Zona Heaster Shue's body to be exhumed and an autopsy conducted. Sure enough, a broken neck was determined to have been the cause of death.

Edward Shue was indicted, tried, and convicted of his wife's murder and sentenced to the West Virginia State Penitentiary, where he died of pneumonia after serving two years. According to the highway marker, Shue's trial was "the only known case in which testimony from a ghost helped convict a murderer."

The case is known locally as the Greenbrier Ghost legend.

Steel-drivin' Myth?

Talcott

Since it was placed on a pedestal in a remote roadside park atop the Great Bend Tunnel on the outskirts of Talcott in 1972, the John Henry statue has endured being peppered with small arms fire, defaced with paint, and dragged by a pickup truck along WV 3. But perhaps the biggest insult that continues to be perpetrated against the life-size bronze monument is a common belief that the larger-than-life person it represents never really existed.

The barrel-chested African-American strongman reportedly outperformed a steam-powered drill in a stone-boring contest in the C&O Railroad's Great Bend Tunnel in the early 1870s. Legend has it that Henry died as a result of his winning, superhuman effort. Since then, the steel-driving, 9-pound hammer-hefting Henry has been the focus of an enduring series of folktales. Songs detailing events in his life have been performed by everyone from Burl Ives to Leadbelly. But is his story truth or fiction?

A statue of the legendary steel driver John Henry stands
watch atop the tunnel he is credited with helping build.

While researching the John Henry phenomenon in the early 1930s,
West Virginia University professor Louis Chappell talked with workers
who had toiled on the Great Bend Tunnel during the time of Henry's
alleged steel-driving feat. Many of them remembered a 6-foot-tall,
200-pound black man named John Henry, although it was unclear

whether he came to Talcott from North Carolina, Virginia, or points farther south. Of the men who remembered Henry, a majority of them recollected that he did indeed engage in a contest with a steam drill. One former C&O worker told Chappell that Brown's foreman and the operator of the mechanical drill had a $100 bet on the outcome of the contest. In recent years several townspeople who have conducted their own research into the John Henry story believe they may have found the site where the steel-driving man is buried.

While it seems likely that a strong, skilled man named John Henry worked on Talcott's Great Bend Tunnel in the 1870s and possibly tested his skills against the rock-drilling abilities of a machine, the notion that Henry died immediately after the feat seems to have little credibility.

The 6,500-foot tunnel Henry reportedly helped carve out has been replaced in recent years by a parallel shaft, the Big Bend Tunnel. An area civic group has bought a tract of land adjacent to the Talcott end of the old tunnel and plans to build a park and museum honoring John Henry. His statue would be moved from its easily vandalized hilltop site to a secure, well-lighted site in the park.

The John Henry statue is located directly atop the entrance to the Big Bend railroad tunnel, just west of Talcott at a small roadside park along WV 3.

Five-Star Bunker
White Sulphur Springs

Mention the word *bunker* in connection with The Greenbrier, West Virginia's world-renowned luxury resort, and the image most likely to be formed is one of a sand trap along the resort's Old White course, where PGA legend Sam Snead once served as pro.

But these days, *bunker* means something entirely different to those familiar with the historic White Sulphur Springs spa. For more than thirty years, conventioneers at The Greenbrier dined, danced, and mingled in the Exhibit Hall in the lower level of the resort's West

Resorting to War

While giving comfort to the enemy is considered an act of treason in some quarters, it was considered an act of diplomatic courtesy by the U.S. Department of State in the days immediately following the Japanese attack on Pearl Harbor and the start of all-out American involvement in World War II.

Less than two weeks after the outbreak of war, 159 German, Italian, Bulgarian, Hungarian, and other Axis diplomats and their families, mainly from Washington's Embassy Row, were rounded up, taken under guard, and sent by train to cool their heels at the legendary Greenbrier resort in White Sulphur Springs. They were later joined at the five-star resort by dozens of other Axis bureaucrats assigned to Washington by their governments.

By March 1942 nearly all of the enemy diplomats and their families had been repatriated home. They apparently found their treatment at the world-renowned resort to be better than adequate: They left tips to the staff totaling $65,000.

After the diplomats left The Greenbrier, the 6,500-acre resort was converted into a hospital for sick and wounded Allied servicemen. Adjacent to the resort, the Army constructed the Ashford Prisoner of War Camp, where about 1,000 former members of General Erwin Rommel's Afrika Korps were interned following their capture in 1943 in North Africa. The German POWs worked at the hospital's laundry and kitchen and helped maintain the grounds.

The Greenbrier returned to its prewar grandeur in 1946, following a major refurbishing. In 1981, thirty-three of the fifty-two American diplomats and embassy personnel who had been held hostage in Iran for 444 days under much less than Greenbrier-like conditions were brought to the White Sulphur Springs resort immediately after their release. Once again, the resort focused its attention on the released hostages' medical care and helped them adjust to freedom and get reacquainted with their families.

Axis diplomats endured house arrest at The Greenbrier during the opening months of World War II. Lawrence Pierce

Virginia Wing, never knowing they were inside a portion of a top-secret relocation facility for members of Congress and their staffs.

When the West Virginia Wing was being built in the late 1950s, officials from the Department of Defense asked the resort's owners to slip the contractor what may have been the biggest change order in state history: Add a 112,000-square-foot, blast-proof, fallout-secure shelter to the original plans for the new wing's basement.

Completed during the height of cold war tensions in 1962, the Greenbrier Bunker was equipped with 30-ton blast doors, reinforced concrete walls, self-contained power and water systems, decon-tamination chambers, a cafeteria, a communications center, and a crematorium. For the members of the U.S. Senate and House of Representatives and the high-ranking staffers it was to serve, the

Members of Congress would have spent the nuclear winter on these basement cots had the cold war turned hot.
Lawrence Pierce

accommodations were not even one star—eighteen dormitories with steel bunk beds, khaki uniforms, and canvas shoes. But its occupants were virtually guaranteed a place in which to comfortably survive for at least sixty days in the event of nuclear holocaust.

While much of the secret facility was kept well out of the public eye, part of it was hidden in plain sight. The display area in the Exhibit Hall was to have served as the work space for congressional staffers, while the convention area's theaters—used for training and motivational presentations in peacetime—had just the right number of seats to accommodate members of Congress in a nuclear attack. A broadcast studio adjacent to the emergency Senate and House chambers had changeable backdrops depicting Washington, D.C., in all seasons, to reassure surviving citizens.

The twelve Department of Defense operatives who maintained the shelter posed as workmen from "Forsyth Associates," a make-believe telephone and television repair contractor.

"Operation Greek Island," as the relocation operation was known, came to an end in 1992, after its presence was made known in a *Washington Post* article. Since 1995 The Greenbrier has operated the Bunker as a tourist attraction, drawing tens of thousands of visitors annually for a chilling glimpse of cold war history.

Ninety-minute tours of the bunker are offered several times daily from spring through fall. The cost is $30 for adults and $15 for children ages ten to eighteen. Reservations are required and may be arranged by calling (800) 624-6070 or (304) 536-7810.

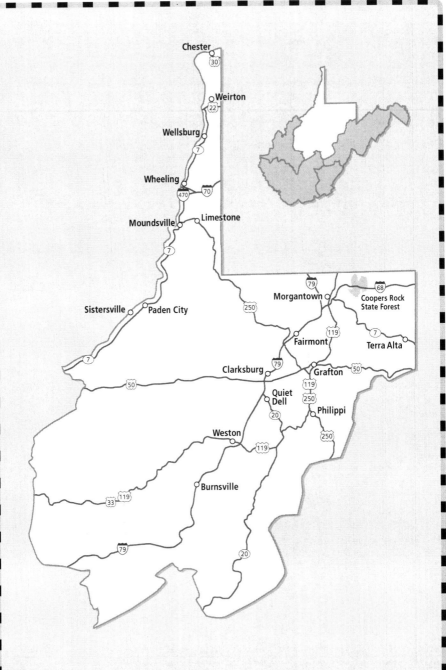

Northern Hills and Northern Panhandle

4

Northern Hills and Northern Panhandle

*D*raw a line from Williamstown on the Ohio River to the western edge of the Allegheny Mountains near Webster Springs and include everything in West Virginia north of that point, and you'll see one constant feature every way you turn: hills, an unbroken chain of hills, seldom more than 1,000 feet high, that stretches all the way to the tip of the Northern Panhandle. The hills are a haven for free thinkers, eccentrics, sports heroes, do-gooders, criminals, and recluses. These hills have stories to tell.

Top Gun
Burnsville

While Jerry West may be West Virginia's best-known homegrown basketball legend, a slender hoops star from tiny Burnsville High School has earned a measure of immortality of his own by setting a national single-game scoring record that has endured for more than a half century. Danny Heater of Burnsville scored 135 points in a contest on January 26, 1960, with Widen, an even smaller high school in neighboring Clay County. The feat, certified by the National Federation of State High School Associations, accounts for the highest point tally ever recorded in a high school, collegiate, or professional basketball game. Heater's score topped Wilt Chamberlain's NBA record 100-point game against New York by 35 points and topped the next-best high school scorer by 7 points.

Prior to the record-setting game against Widen, the 6-foot, 1-inch, 145-pound senior was known more for being shy than a showboat and for his willingness to pass to a teammate with a better look at the basket. In fact, during his 135-point run, he also managed to bring in 32 rebounds and make 7 assists. Heater was averaging a noteworthy 27 points a game going into the Widen game. But his coach wanted him to try for the state record, which then stood at 74 points, to garner his star player enough attention to draw the interest of a collegiate scout. For Heater, the son of a laid-off coal miner, playing basketball at the next level offered him what was likely his only shot at a college education.

Heater did get a chance to play at Richmond, but not on a basketball scholarship. A former state senator paid his way to attend the university, but a homesick Heater returned to Burnsville after six weeks in the Virginia capital.

In an interview forty years after the 173–43 victory, Heater said he had mixed feelings about setting the record. "I was happy and sad at the same time," he said, happy for having his team recognized for a scoring record and sad for humiliating the Widen team.

"I wasn't raised to embarrass people," he said. "I didn't know what to say. What do you say when you've done that to somebody?"

After working in a clerical position for the FBI, Heater went on to a career as a Delta ticket agent in Washington, D.C.

Titanic Teapot

Chester

The self-proclaimed "World's Largest Teapot" began its career in the root beer trade.

In 1938 William "Babe" Devon, the operator of a Chester pottery outlet store, bought a huge wooden barrel in Pennsylvania that had

A modified root beer barrel is now the world's largest teapot.

been used in Hires Root Beer advertising. He added a spout, handle, and lid and topped the lid with a large glass ball to serve as the knob. Local youths were hired to operate a souvenir shop and refreshment stand inside the teapot, which was placed along busy WV 2.

The stand went through various owners and occasional abandonment over the years until 1990, when the Chester City Council voted to restore the teapot and move it to a site adjacent to the intersection of WV 2 and US 30, near the Jennings Randolph Bridge over the Ohio River. New tin was added, the spout was replaced with a replica of the original, and the original paint scheme was restored with fresh coats of red and white.

The titanic crockery replica is 14 feet in diameter and stands 14 feet tall. Its restoration helps call attention to Chester's importance as a pottery hub. The Homer Laughlin China Co., located about 1 mile downriver at Newell, was once the world's largest pottery maker and accounted for 10 percent of all U.S. production. It remains the biggest domestic pottery producer and is known mainly for its colorful art deco-style Fiesta dinnerware that is used and collected worldwide.

The teapot can be seen in a small fenced park adjacent to the Jennings Randolph Bridge ramp near the intersection of WV 2 and US 30 in Chester, West Virginia's northernmost town—32 miles northwest of Pittsburgh, Pennsylvania.

Men in Black
Clarksburg

The mysterious "Men in Black," the intimidating government officials who, according to UFO conspiracy theorists, browbeat into silence those who have had close encounters with aliens, have roots in West Virginia.

Gray Barker, a lifelong resident of the Mountain State, first brought the black suit-wearing, black sedan-driving G-men, made popular by

Tommy Lee Jones and Will Smith, to public attention in his book *They Knew Too Much about Flying Saucers.*

Barker, born and raised in Braxton County, went to college at Glenville State College and later carved out a career writing about UFOs, extraterrestrials, and other paranormal topics.

Barker's 1956 book was based on events that allegedly happened to the editor of a UFO-themed magazine Barker wrote for, who suddenly shut down his magazine and international flying saucer tracking bureau after allegedly being ordered to do so by black-clad government agents.

Barker wrote two more books dealing with Men in Black. The last was *MIB: The Secret Terror among Us,* which was released in 1984, the year of Barker's death.

Among Barker's other works was *The Silver Bridge,* a book released in 1970, which linked the collapse of the Silver Bridge over the Ohio River at Point Pleasant, West Virginia, in 1967 with the alleged appearance of the otherworldly creature Mothman (see previous entry "Mothman Lives!") in the Point Pleasant area. *The Silver Bridge* came out five years before John Keel's *The Mothman Prophecies,* on which the Richard Gere movie of the same name was based.

While Barker made a name for himself writing about UFOs, aliens, and paranormal activity, he was apparently privately skeptical of such phenomena. Some writers have suggested that he was involved in one or more hoaxes involving UFOs.

When not writing about otherworldly matters, Barker worked as a theatrical film booker in Clarksburg. Many of his writings are preserved in the Clarksburg–Harrison County Public Library's special exhibits section at Waldomore, the former mansion that stands next to the main library complex at 404 Pike Street in downtown Clarksburg. For details, call (304) 627-2236, or visit www.clarksburglibrary .info/waldomore.

★ ★

Mark the Lion Hearted

Coopers Rock

When it's time for Mark Jenkins to feed his cats, he bypasses the kibbles and goes straight for the deer legs. Visitors should refrain from petting Jenkins's felines at such times, unless they're in the market for a new nickname—something like Lefty or Stubby.

Jenkins operates Coopers Rock Mountain Lion Sanctuary, a U.S. Fish and Wildlife Service–licensed home for orphaned, abandoned, and abused mountain lions (also known as cougars, catamounts, and pumas, depending on the region) from across the nation. Mountain lions placed in Jenkins's care by wildlife officials from Montana to Maryland live in large, secure outdoor enclosures that incorporate as many natural landscape features as possible.

The call of the wild is frequently heard at the mountain lion sanctuary at Coopers Rock. Lawrence Pierce

* *

Thousands of schoolchildren visit the sanctuary annually to learn more about the food chain–topping predators. While drop-in visits are discouraged, Jenkins can arrange tours with advance notice.

Jenkins, a graduate of nearby West Virginia University, and his wife, Sheila, developed an interest in the large, potentially lethal felines in the '90s, while they were both working at a wildlife park in the Southeast.

Their oldest resident is Burton, who was fourteen months old when he arrived at the sanctuary from a private zoo in the Southeast not long after the sanctuary opened in 1998.

The sanctuary, located in deep woods along a mountain creek at the end of a long country road, has space for only four or five mountain lions. The setting is also the home of the Jenkins's Mountain Creek Cabins retreat, a cluster of seven comfortable, well-appointed log cabins, where guests can arrange private tours of the sanctuary.

Mountain lions once had a statewide presence in West Virginia, but now they are believed to be extinct—although enough sightings, scat, and tracks turn up from time to time to suggest that previously domesticated big cats have been released in the wild here.

For details on the Coopers Rock Mountain Lion Sanctuary, visit www.cougarsanctuary.org. For more information on Mountain Creek Cabins, call (866) 379-7548, or visit www.mountaincreekcabins.com.

First Fatality

Grafton

In May 1861, just weeks after Confederate artillery fire on Fort Sumter launched the Civil War, Private Thornsberry Bailey Brown posed for a photograph wearing a pistol in his belt and a look of grim determination on his face, seemingly fully prepared to play his role in a historic undertaking.

As it turned out, his role was one he likely wished someone else had played—to become the first Union combat death in the bloody struggle.

On a Roll

If it's got a grease slick running through it, you know it's real.

The pepperoni roll, an all–West Virginia delicacy, began as a simple miners' lunch in the north-central West Virginia coalfields in the 1930s. Since then, it has become a staple on convenience store counters across the state.

Rarely seen outside West Virginia, pepperoni rolls are produced by a handful of small bakeries within a 50-mile radius of Fairmont, where they were first commercially prepared. The basic pepperoni roll is a yeasty, 6- to 10-inch white roll, in which a thick-sliced, rectangular wedge of pepperoni long enough to jut out both ends is inserted

Infused with a pepperoni wedge and grease, this northern West Virginia delicacy has spread statewide.
Lawrence Pierce.

and baked. Juices from the baking pepperoni stick percolate into the roll, giving it its unique flavor and leaving a trademark grease layer on the bottom of the dough.

Fairmont's Country Club Bakery has been making the lunchtime favorite longer than any other producer. Its founder, Frank Argiro, a former coal miner, was aware that many of his fellow workers brought loaves of bread and pepperoni sticks in their dinner buckets for a simple underground meal. He decided to try slicing the spiced meat into smaller sticks and baking them within the bread, to make a meal that could be handled easier and neater than a sandwich. His rolls became popular enough that he gave up mining in favor of baking and opened the Country Club Bakery, which is still in operation at 1211 Country Club Road in Fairmont (304-363-5690) and still specializing in pepperoni rolls.

Several variations on the roll have evolved over the decades, the most common being the addition of peppered cheese to the pepperoni stick filling.

For those not dining underground, pepperoni rolls are sometimes split open, filled with stewed green peppers, and sprinkled with mozzarella before being broiled until the cheese melts. Pepperoni rolls are often sold during fund-raisers for youth groups, giving buyers a spicy option to Girl Scout cookies.

Killed in action two days after enlisting, Thornsberry Bailey
Brown now rests in Grafton National Cemetery.

As a member of the newly formed Grafton Guards, soon to
become Company B of the Second West Virginia Infantry, Brown was
assigned to a federal encampment at Pruntytown in Taylor County. In
nearby Fetterman, a freshly arrived Confederate force was assigned to
control a section of the Baltimore & Ohio Railroad and recruit troops.

On the night of May 22, two days after his enlistment and forty
days after the official outbreak of war, Private Brown and Lieutenant
Daniel Wilson were walking along the Northwestern Turnpike, now
US 50, from Pruntytown toward Grafton when they encountered
a Confederate checkpoint. When ordered to halt by Private Daniel

Knight, Brown instead drew his pistol and fired, nicking the rebel soldier in the ear. Knight returned fire with a musket, killing Brown outright with a blast to his chest.

Brown's death occurred two days before Colonel Elmer Ephraim Ellsworth was killed in Alexandria, Virginia, in a dispute over the removal of a Confederate flag. Ellsworth, an officer and a campaign aide to President Abraham Lincoln, is often credited with being the first Union combat casualty.

Ten days after Brown was struck down, the Civil War's first land battle involving organized troops took place in nearby Barbour County, where a force of 800 Confederate troops threatened B&O Railroad operations there. On June 3, 1861, nearly 3,000 Union troops under Colonel Benjamin Kelley and Colonel Ebenezer Dumont drove out the southern troops in a surprise attack that became known as the "Philippi Races."

While no one was killed in the rout, twenty-six Confederate and four Union soldiers were wounded, including two southern soldiers struck by artillery fire who became the war's first amputees. The first was Private J. E. Hanger, who enlisted the day before the battle and had his leg struck by a 6-pound cannonball. A Union surgeon amputated the limb, using a ripped-out barn door as an operating table. Anxious to walk again after being furloughed home, Hanger designed and made a hinged prosthetic leg that bent at the knee and ankle, which he patented and later made available to other injured veterans. Today Hanger Orthopedic is the world's largest provider of prosthetic patient care services, treating more than 650,000 patients annually.

Maternal Flame
Grafton

While some skeptics credit the greeting card lobby or a cabal of florists with creating Mother's Day, the unofficial holiday that fans the flames of love and guilt traces its roots to a church in the timeworn railroad town of Grafton.

Grafton's International Mother's Day Shrine and Museum is a tribute to the creator of the holiday beloved by Hallmark.

It was there, on May 10, 1908, in Andrews Methodist Episcopal Church, under the direction of Anna Jarvis, that the nation's first Mother's Day service was held. Born just south of town in a two-story frame house occupied by Union Army leader General George McClellan in the early days of the Civil War, Jarvis conceived of the observance to honor her mother, Ann Jarvis. During the final year of the war, Ann Jarvis organized a group of mothers from both Confederate and Union families to help tend to wounded soldiers from both sides. After the war she organized events to reunite war-torn Grafton by bringing together families of opposing wartime loyalties.

The first Mother's Day observance came three years after Ann Jarvis's death, at the church where she taught Sunday school for twenty years. Anna Jarvis introduced the idea of using the white carnation to symbolize the observance and developed texts and visual tools to promote the event.

West Virginia governor William Glasscock issued the first Mother's Day proclamation in 1910, and at a national Methodist conference in Minneapolis in 1912, Anna Jarvis was recognized as the founder of Mother's Day. Two years later President Woodrow Wilson signed into law a resolution designating the second Sunday in May as Mother's Day.

Andrews Methodist Episcopal Church at 11 Main Street in downtown Grafton now houses the International Mother's Day Shrine and Museum, dedicated to preserving the legacy of Ann Jarvis and the spirit of motherhood everywhere. The shrine and museum are open from 10:00 a.m. to 4:00 p.m., Tuesday through Saturday, April through October. For more information, contact the International Mother's Day Shrine Foundation at info@mothersdayshrine.com.

Panhandle Palace
Limestone

West Virginia's version of the Taj Mahal looms into view unexpectedly, after following a winding, 4-mile drive along a potholed, one-and-a-half-lane-wide country road, prompting more than one first-time visitor to mutter, "Holy cow!"

It's an appropriate expletive, since there are plenty of holy cows in the pastures surrounding Prabhupada's Palace of Gold, a temple built by Krishna Consciousness devotees over the course of seven years to honor their faith's founder, Srila Prabhupada. The New Vrindaban community, which built and maintains the palace, also operates the Goraksa Seva Cow Protection Program, which gives lifetime grazing rights to the community's retired milk cows and their male offspring.

A Hare Krishna swami's vision is brought to life on a
West Virginia ridgetop.

When work on the palace began in 1972, the intention was to
build a home for Srila Prabhubada, who came to love New Vrindaban
after spending two months in an aging farmhouse there in 1969,
with a small group of Hare Krishna devotees who became the nucleus
of the community.

But the size and scope of the project changed dramatically, as the
untrained devotees who built the structure, often through trial-and-
error techniques, improvised and embellished construction plans.
What evolved was a grand palace of marble, teak, stained glass, crystal chandeliers, landscaped gardens, and more than 8,000 square feet
of 22-carat gold leaf trim.

Prabhupada died before he had the chance to move into the
ridgetop palace, which became a memorial to his work—and a major

tourist attraction, drawing nearly 100,000 visitors a year during the community's heyday in the 1980s. But a series of scandals rocked New Vrindaban, ranging from racketeering charges for selling T-shirts and other items without obtaining needed licensing agreements, to sexual abuse of students in the community-run school and the murder of a devotee.

New Vrindaban was temporarily banned from being a part of the international Hare Krishna organization before its leadership changed and its focus returned to being a learning center for Krishna Consciousness.

At its peak more than 1,000 devotees lived at New Vrindaban, and the Northern Panhandle Hare Krishna community was one of the largest in the world. In addition to dairy cattle and work horses, the 4,000-acre community was for several years the home of Malini, West Virginia's sole resident elephant.

The community has been fully restored to the international organization and draws thousands of Hindu visitors for religious holiday festivals and celebrations, as well as curious secular tourists.

To reach New Vrindaban from Wheeling, take Exit 2 off I-270, and turn right at the end of the exit ramp. Follow that road a short distance to its intersection with WV 88. Turn right and follow WV 88 south for 8 miles, where it ends at an intersection with US 250. Turn left on US 250 and follow it south 1.5 miles, then turn left on Palace Road/Limestone Hill Road. Follow it for 3.7 miles to the Palace of Gold.

For information on Palace of Gold tours, call (304) 843-1812, or visit www.palaceofgold.com/tourist.

Barney's Fifedom

Morgantown

Barney Fife, Mayberry's backwoods deputy sheriff on *The Andy Griffith Show*, may have been bumbling, self-important, and nearly always wrong, but the actor who portrayed him is revered in his West Virginia hometown.

Driverless Transit

Having a rapid transit system that carries 16,000 people a day over a hilly, 8.2-mile route—all without a driver—doesn't raise an eyebrow for the students, staff, and faculty at West Virginia University who ride it. The futuristic system, designed by Boeing Aerospace, has been around for more than thirty years and is as familiar a part of the campus landscape as the Mountainlair student union or the clam-shaped WVU Coliseum.

Morgantown's Personal Rapid Transit system, which opened in 1975, was designed to connect sections of WVU's sprawling campus by automated people-moving cars traveling on concrete guideways, most of them elevated to pass above streets. Without it, traffic problems in the already congested college town of steep hills, narrow streets, and

Drivers aren't needed to steer Personal Rapid Transit cars through West Virginia University's hilly Morgantown campus.
West Virginia University

overpriced housing would be unimaginable. The Morgantown PRT was the first in a series of five automated people-mover systems built across the nation in the 1970s and 1980s by the U.S. Department of Transportation as urban transit demonstration projects.

WVU students, faculty, and staff ride the system by swiping magnetically coded ID cards through turnstiles at the PRT's five stations. Other passengers pay a 50-cent fee. Upon entering a station, passengers press a button indicating the station to which they are traveling and go to a specific platform to await the next car headed to that stop. Overhead signs show the destination of the next arriving car.

Each of the system's seventy-three electric-powered cars has room for eight seated passengers, with additional pole-equipped standing room for twelve. The passenger load increases significantly during WVU's annual Mountaineer Week celebration, which includes a Mountaineer Cram event. In 2000 a record ninety-seven individuals squeezed themselves into a PRT car.

During peak hours cars are dispatched as needed to take passengers to their desired stations, at speeds up to 30 miles per hour, bypassing stations in between. On nights and weekends the cars are programmed to stop at every station. This individualized destination option makes the Morgantown PRT unique in the small world of people-moving transit systems.

City and university officials hope to extend the line into Morgantown's wharf district along the Monongahela, where a variety of shops, restaurants, and hiking-biking trails can be found.

Considered a white elephant in its early years due to major cost overruns and delays, the system operates on a break-even basis and is studied by transit experts from around the world.

For more on the PRT, visit www.transportation.wvu.edu, or call (304) 293-5011.

Morgantown's version of the Walk of Stars includes but one entry so far: hometown hero Don Knotts.

Follow Don Knotts Boulevard along the Monongahela River through downtown Morgantown, hang a right on Fayette Street, then turn right again on High Street, and you'll find the Don Knotts star embedded in the sidewalk in front of the Metropolitan Theater. The Greater Morgantown Community Trust has established a Don Knotts Legacy Fund to erect a Don Knotts statue in a Don Knotts Memorial Park between Don Knotts Boulevard and the Monongahela River.

Born July 24, 1924, in Morgantown, Knotts graduated from his hometown college, West Virginia University, with a degree in theater. He went on to hit the stand-up comic circuit, appear in radio dramas and sitcoms, and perform with Andy Griffith in the Broadway and movie versions of *No Time for Sergeants* in the 1950s.

In 1960 he teamed up with Griffith again to launch *The Andy Griffith Show,* where he achieved cult status with his portrayal of Barney Fife, Griffith's overconfident but clueless deputy, for which he earned five Emmy awards.

Knotts, who racked up dozens of film credits and another sitcom or two after leaving *The Andy Griffith Show,* died in 2006 but lives on in memories—and reruns. It's no coincidence that the local branch of the Andy Griffith Show Rerun Watchers' Club is known as Barney's Hometown Chapter.

Morgantown's Walk of Fame, featuring the Don Knotts star, can be found at 369 High Street.

Profound Mound
Moundsville

It took a mountain of work to create the largest conical burial mound in North America near Grave Creek's confluence with the Ohio River a little more than 2,000 years ago.

In fact, archaeologists estimate that it took the Adena people about one hundred years to carry 57,000 tons of soil in more than one million basket loads to create the 70-foot-tall cone.

Many early settlers who viewed the mound and the moatlike trench that surrounded it concluded that Native Americans could not have created such an impressive monument, or "remarkable artificial mound of earth," as Corps of Discovery coleader Meriwether Lewis described it in 1803.

Lost cultures from the Old World, the Lost Tribe of Israel, and a race of moon-eyed giants with red beards were all speculated to have built the mound, until it was partially excavated in 1838 by amateur archaeologists who tunneled into it and found two burial vaults. The bodies of three Indians were found in the vaults, along with thousands of shell beads and five copper bracelets.

In an early attempt to convert the mound into a tourist attraction, area residents built a three-story observatory atop the earthwork in the 1840s and added a saloon and dance stage in the 1850s. The structures were removed after each venture failed to draw travelers.

The state of West Virginia bought the mound in 1909 but did little with it until after World War II, when a small museum was built at the base of the monument. Since then the Delf Norona Museum has been built at the site and was recently expanded to include storage space for archaeological materials from sites across the state.

The Grave Creek Mound Archaeological Complex is located at 801 Jefferson Avenue, Moundsville. For more information, call (304) 843-4128.

North America's largest burial mound took a century to build but entombed just three bodies.

Doing Leisure Time
Moundsville

If any place deserves to be haunted, it's the West Virginia Penitentiary in Moundsville.

Between its opening in 1876 and its court-ordered closing in 1995, 85 of its inmates were executed by hanging; 9 were put to death in "Old Sparky," the inmate-built electric chair; and another 998 died of shanking, suicide, or old age. The dark, Gothic-style stone fortress was originally built to hold 450 inmates but at times warehoused as many as 2,400.

The prison had been open only ten years when the *Cincinnati Enquirer* described it as "hell on earth," where inmates were subjected to "cruel, brutish treatment."

Before courts ruled that serving a sentence in a 5-by-7-foot cell in the aging prison constituted cruel and unusual punishment, there were riots, hostage takings, and incidents of arson.

These days, the Moundsville Economic Development Council operates the prison as a tourist attraction, using former corrections officers as guides. The ninety-minute tours include displays of inmate-crafted weapons and works of art, a close-up look at Old Sparky, visits to the vividly painted cells of psychopathic lifers, and a letter from Charles Manson asking the penitentiary's warden to allow him to serve out the rest of his life sentence in Moundsville—located just a few miles from a childhood home.

Among the 30,000 people who visit the prison annually are ghost hunters, who pay $60 for overnight stays within the prison, where shadowy apparitions and unexplained voices and noises are frequently reported. The entry fee includes pizza and a movie, presumably a scary one.

The prison was featured in *Fools' Parade,* the 1971 movie starring James Stewart, George Kennedy, and a young Kurt Russell, and it depicts a decrepit Mexican prison in the opening scenes of the 2010 martial arts film *Warrior,* starring former Charleston resident Nick

★ ★

Tourists now do time in the tiers of barred cages that once contained the state's most hardened criminals. Lawrence Pierce

Nolte. Several cable television shows dealing with the paranormal, including The Travel Channel's *Ghost Hunters* and MTV's *Fear,* have been filmed here as well.

Each year since 1997 the prison has been the scene of a mock riot, sponsored by the National Institute of Justice and the West Virginia High Technology Foundation. In recent years the four-day event has drawn more than 1,500 participants from forty states and eight foreign countries.

Daytime historic tours at the prison are held April through November, Tuesday through Sunday, from 11:00 a.m. to 4:00 p.m. The cost is $10 for adults, $8 for seniors, and $5 for kids ages six and older.

Overnight ghost tours sell out quickly and are booked months, sometimes years, in advance.

For details, call (304) 845-6200, or visit www.wvpentours.com.

Marble Mecca
Paden City

West Virginia may be eccentric in dozens of ways, but it hasn't lost its marbles.

Marble King, a small factory in the Ohio River town of Paden City, cranks out more than one million marbles a day for youthful marble shooters, collectors, board game players, and aerosol spray can users. It is one of only two marble manufacturers still operating in the United States. Marble King makes use of 4.5 tons of recycled glass each day of production. The crushed glass is fed into a handmade

Paden City's Marble King uses recycled glass to roll out up to one million marbles a day.

brick furnace that's heated to 2,300 degrees Fahrenheit to liquefy the material so that it can be rolled into spherical orbs.

Since 1968 Marble King has cosponsored the National Marbles Tournament in Wildwood, New Jersey. Each year the best youthful marble shooters, or "mibsters," from across the nation compete in the event.

The Marble King factory and its interactive museum and gift shop are located just off WV 2, Paden City's main drag. Call (800) 672-5564 for details.

Mummies Dearest
Philippi

Located near the historic Philippi covered bridge in a restored railroad depot, the Barbour County Historical Society Museum offers visitors displays of Civil War artifacts, pioneer farm and household implements—and the mummified remains of two former mental patients.

Despite Philippi's role as the site of the first land battle of the Civil War and the home of the largest and oldest covered bridge in the state, it's the Philippi mummies who are the museum's star attractions.

In 1888 Graham Hamrick, a local farmer and storekeeper with a fascination for Egyptology, acquired the corpses of two women from the state mental hospital in nearby Weston. Hamrick had developed a preservation system that he had used with success on snakes, vegetables, and small mammals and eventually planned to apply for a patent for use on humans. His mummification process worked well enough on the two recently departed mental patients that showman P. T. Barnum arranged to take them on a tour of Europe in 1891.

Hamrick patented his mummification formula the following year and displayed his preserved prototypes at every opportunity, but he failed to cash in on his patented process, despite its success. The mummies were donated to the museum in 1985, after being swept out of their temporary quarters in a devastating flood and receiving some touch-up work from a local mortician.

The Bluebeard of Quiet Dell

Having Robert Mitchum portray a guy from a small northern West Virginia town who went on to gain national recognition in his chosen field would ordinarily be a good thing. But in the 1955 Charles Laughton film *The Night of the Hunter*, Mitchum plays the role of serial killer Harry Powers, a Quiet Dell used furniture dealer who traveled the nation in the 1920s in a quest to separate lonely widows from their money and their lives.

Powers, whose real name was Herman Drenth, was brought to justice in 1931 after relatives of a missing Illinois woman long overdue home from a visit with the short, pudgy West Virginia man became suspicious and alerted authorities. At about the same time, a neighbor reported an unpleasant aroma wafting from Powers's property and reported it to police. Inside a shed on Powers's property, investigators found two rooms, one in which Powers gassed his victims to death and an adjacent room with a window through which Powers watched his victims die.

In a ditch outside the building, police dug up the bodies of the missing woman and her three children, as well as the remains of the widow Dorothy Lemke of Worcester, Massachusetts. Inside Powers's house, they found a quantity of form-style letters ready to send out to widows who had joined lonely hearts "pen pal" clubs.

While investigators believe Powers/Drenth may have killed fifty or more women, he only admitted to killing the five individuals found on his property. "You got me on five," he told investigators. "What good would fifty more do?"

Some critics consider Mitchum's portrayal of Powers/Drenth in *The Night of the Hunter* to have been his finest cinematic performance. A number of scenes from the movie were shot in Moundsville, the childhood home of Davis Grubb, who wrote the novel on which the film was based.

Powers/Drenth told police he watched his victims die from his window-equipped "operations room" because it gave him a thrill that "beat any cathouse I was ever in." He was hanged on March 18, 1932, at the West Virginia Penitentiary in Moundsville.

The mummies and Hamrick's story were featured in a 2002 segment of National Geographic's *The Mummy Road Show.* But recently their display has come under fire from a national mental health organization that considers it not only undignified, but "shocking and horrifying" as well, and wants the mummies to be buried.

But the mummies remain on display in glass cases in a converted restroom in the former train depot, where information about Hamrick's mummification process can also be found, as part of the $1 admission fee to the mummy wing.

The Barbour County Historical Society Museum is located at 200 North Main Street in downtown Philippi. Hours are 11:00 a.m. to 4:00 p.m. Monday through Saturday, 1:00 to 4:00 p.m. Sunday, May through October. Call (304) 457-4846, or visit www.philippi.org for more information.

Ferry Godfather
Sistersville

The oldest ferry still plying the murky waters of the Ohio River doesn't operate on a set schedule, but the service is quick and easy to use: If the boat is on the Ohio shore when you arrive at the Sistersville ferry landing, just pull your vehicle down to the ramp and look like you may want to cross. Soon the ferry will be chugging its way toward you, a deckhand on the bow ready to open the boarding gate.

In operation since 1815 with time-outs for the Civil War and an eleven-month break in service in 1990–1991 while a replacement vessel was bought and outfitted, the Sistersville ferry connects the former oil and gas boomtown of Sistersville with the tiny, unincorporated burg of Fly, Ohio. More importantly, the ferry connects WV 2 with Ohio's Route 7, at a point where the nearest bridge is 17 miles away, north or south. Commuting factory workers, teachers, and deliverymen can save up to thirty minutes of driving time by taking the eight-minute ride on the ferry.

★ ★

The Sistersville ferry is the only service still operating along the 277-mile stretch of river separating West Virginia from Ohio. It generally runs from April to November, but if the weather and passenger numbers cooperate, it has been known to open in March and operate until Christmas Eve. Hours are 6:00 a.m. to 6:00 p.m., seven days a week. The fare is $3 for cars, $2 for motorcycles, and $1 for pedestrians.

Sightseers often outnumber commuters on the boat in the fall, when foliage displays in the Ohio Valley can be spectacular. Since the boat crosses the midpoint of the 20-mile "Long Reach," the longest straight stretch on the Ohio River, views from the deck can cover several miles of valley.

The ferry is owned by the city of Sistersville. For more information, call (304) 652-6361.

For the best eight-minute cruise in 277 miles, take the historic Sistersville ferry to Fly, Ohio.

Cheesed at Marconi
Terra Alta

For boosters of the former Terra Alta dentist Mahlon Loomis, getting historians to back their contention that Loomis was the true inventor of the radio is like pulling teeth.

In 1866, eight years before Guglielmo Marconi was born, Loomis successfully demonstrated what he called "wireless telegraphy" by making a galvanometer on one wire-screened kite cause a meter on a similar kite 14 miles distant to move by grounding a copper wire attached to the first kite.

According to the U.S. Library of Congress, the feat marked "the first known instance of wireless aerial communication."

Loomis duplicated the feat four years later on two Navy ships anchored 2 miles apart in Chesapeake Bay. But was it radio?

Not exactly, according to scientific consensus.

Loomis, Heinrich Hertz, and Nikolai Tesla all have supporters who argue that they should be credited with inventing radio, but after examining and reexamining the facts, Marconi still appears to deserve his inventor's status.

Loomis did make some groundbreaking achievements, in addition to making the first wireless aerial communication. As early as 1864, while the Civil War was still raging, he envisioned "a process by which telegraphic communications may be made across the ocean without any wires."

He patented a general theory of wireless telegraphy and later induced Congress to charter, but never fund, the Loomis Aerial Tele-graph Co., to carry out further experiments in wireless communica-tion. He was the first to use a complete antenna and ground system.

Loomis died in Terra Alta in 1886, nine years before Marconi was credited with inventing the radio. According to an account by his brother, George, Loomis said he was aware many considered him a crank or a fool for believing in the possibilities of wireless telegra-phy. "But I know that I am right," Loomis said. "And if the present generation lives long enough, their opinions will be changed—and their wonder will be that they did not perceive it before. I shall never see it perfected—but it will be—and others will have the honor of the discovery."

A state highway marker along WV 7 about 5 miles west of the West Virginia–Maryland border marks the cemetery where Loomis, the "forerunner of wireless telegraphy," is buried.

Border-to-Border Town
Weirton

Steel was such a big business in the Northern Panhandle city of Weirton that by the time the 1950s rolled around, the town had expanded so much that it stretched from the Ohio border in the west all the way to the Pennsylvania state line to the east. Of course, that part of

Take a walk across West Virginia at Weirton, which starts at the Ohio border and ends at the Pennsylvania line.

West Virginia is only about 4 miles wide, but it's still unusual to have a single town span the width of a state.

The Pittsburgh industrialist E. T. Weir brought his steel-making business to a stretch of the Ohio River encompassing part of present-day Weirton in 1909 and soon had ten mills up and running. An influx of workers needed to operate the new factories caused the town to expand rapidly inland from the West Virginia shore of the Ohio River. When the 1940s arrived, four towns in the vicinity of the steel mills had grown to the point that they practically touched. The communities merged in 1947, creating the new municipality of Weirton, which grew to include 28,000 people by 1970, when Weirton Steel was the nation's fifth-largest steel producer.

In 1977 the town was the setting for many scenes in the movie *The Deer Hunter,* which starred Robert De Niro and Christopher Walken. The trailer where De Niro's character lived was located on the west side of Main Street.

Weirton is the only city in the United States that is situated in one state while its borders touch two other states.

One-of-a-Kind Peacemaker
Weirton

An experimental cold war–era U.S. Army tank, the only one of its kind ever produced, never saw duty in the field, but it continues to keep Communists at bay at the western city limits of Weirton.

The T95E tank, developed about 1960, was a hybrid that made use of an American chassis and a British turret, according to a sign at the Brooke-Hancock Veterans Memorial Park, where the tank overlooks the Ohio River and the US 22 bridge. Perhaps the tank was never mass-produced because its British half wanted to roll down the left side of the battlefield, while the American half favored the right.

Although the T95 employed a laserlike rangefinder and made use of a refined armor system, Pentagon officials opted to scrap the model and go with an updated version of the Patton tank.

The T95E, the only tank of its kind ever built, keeps enemies at bay at Weirton's Brooke-Hancock Veterans Memorial Park.

Other eye-catching pieces of military hardware at the park are an A-7D Corsair II fighter-bomber, a Marine Cobra helicopter gunship, two artillery pieces, and an antiaircraft gun. The park is located adjacent to the US 22 on- and off-ramps at the western end of Weirton.

Corps of Discovery's Last Man Standing

Wellsburg

After joining the Virginia militia and fighting Indians along the upper Ohio River Valley from a fort at Wheeling during the early 1790s, Patrick Gass decided he needed a break. He joined a flatboat crew heading downriver to New Orleans, sailed to Cuba, then on to Philadelphia, and ended up in Mercersburg, Pennsylvania, where he worked as a carpenter on the home of future president James Buchanan's father.

Brain Stormer

If you were a patient in Weston State Hospital or any other West Virginia state mental hospital during the 1950s, and Dr. Walter Freeman said he wanted to pick your brain, he probably meant it literally.

The neurologist was best known for developing the transorbital lobotomy, a procedure in which an ice pick–like probe is hammered into a patient's eye socket, then twisted to sever the nerve connections between the thalamus and frontal lobes. During the 1940s and '50s, Freeman performed thousands of the procedures, designed to reduce violent and self-destructive behavior, in hospitals across the nation. But nowhere was his handiwork more evident than in West Virginia, where cash-strapped hospital officials viewed transorbital lobotomies as the fastest and most cost-effective way to get patients' behavior stabilized enough to send them home.

With the backing of mental health officials, Freeman launched his "West Virginia Project" in July 1952, during which he performed a record 228 transorbital lobotomies in two weeks at four state mental hospitals, including twenty-four procedures in a single day. A dose of electroshock therapy was the only anesthetic used during the ice pick treatments, which usually lasted about ten minutes. Through his own data, Freeman determined that an improvement occurred in only one of every three patients he lobotomized, but he continued to perform the procedures long after they fell out of vogue with the advent of effective therapeutic drugs. He performed his last two lobotomies on the same day in 1967. One of the patients seemed to respond favorably to the procedure, while the other died a few days later.

Patrick Gass lived life large until he died at age ninety-nine.

But Gass quickly became restless with a carpenter's life, so he enlisted in the U.S. Army in 1799 and was sent to Fort Kaskaskia on the Mississippi River in Illinois Territory. In the fall of 1803, Meriwether Lewis and William Clark stopped at the fort to seek recruits for their historic westward expedition. Gass told Lewis and Clark he was their man and left the Illinois country to head up the Missouri River and into the history books.

At the age of thirty-three, Gass was one of the oldest enlisted men to join the Corps of Discovery and was only ten months younger than Clark, the party's second-most senior member, behind blacksmith John Shields, who was thirty-five. When another Fort Kaskaskia recruit, Charles Floyd, died of appendicitis early in the journey, the expedition's enlisted men elected Gass their sergeant. Gass took charge of building the expedition's winter quarters and led the expedition while Lewis and Clark took side trips to explore and collect.

Six months after the epic journey had ended, Gass published an account of the expedition based on his journal entries. His book came out seven years before the official Lewis and Clark account. Gass returned to what is now West Virginia, settling in the Ohio River town of Wellsburg, where he worked as a ferry operator, among other jobs, before reenlisting to fight in the War of 1812. He returned to Wellsburg after the war and in 1831, at the age of sixty, married eighteen-year-old Maria Hamilton, the daughter of a Wellsburg magistrate. The couple lived on a hillside farm in a log home Gass built and raised five children.

Gass outlived not only his wife, who died in 1847, but every other member of the Lewis and Clark expedition, including Sacagawea's baby, Jean Baptiste Charbonneau. When he died at the age of ninety-nine, he had voted for eighteen presidents and seen the unexplored Oregon country reached by the Corps of Discovery achieve statehood.

Gass's tombstone can be seen near the top of the hillside in Brooke Cemetery in Wellsburg, located a short distance off WV 2.

Stumping for Free Speech
Weston

When a storm severely damaged a silver maple in front of Eric Spelsburg's Center Street home, the Weston man was left with a dilemma about what to do with the remaining 4-foot-tall stump.

After watching a television segment dealing with election season stump speeches, he solved the problem by using American ingenuity and a few other basic tools to turn an eyesore into an all-American tribute to the right of free speech.

Anyone is welcome to use the Weston Free Speech Stump, which now features a railed stairway leading to a stump-top platform. Area candidates have taken to delivering stump speeches from its not-so-lofty heights.

The Weston Free Speech Stump is located at the corner of Center and East Fifth Streets in downtown Weston.

A stump speech is yours for the asking
at Weston's Free Speech Stump.

Government Robbery
Weston

Why raise taxes to fund a new state government when you can legally
rob a bank?

That was the unassailable logic pursued by the founders of the
Reorganized Government of Virginia, a group formed during the early
days of the Civil War that favored carving out a new Union-aligned
state from Virginia's western counties. While many people know West
Virginia's statehood was a product of the Civil War, few are aware
that swag from a Union Army bank heist in the Lewis County town of
Weston was used to finance the state's transitional government.

The robbery that financed West Virginia's new government took place at this Weston landmark. Kenny Kemp

The robbery took place on June 30, 1861, a few days after the Weston merchant Presley M. Hale, a Unionist supporting the Reorganized Government, told the Union general George McClellan, then stationed in Grafton, about a horde of gold coins being kept in the Exchange Bank of Weston. The money was being held to pay for the completion of a new state mental hospital, the Trans-Allegheny Lunatic Asylum (see the entry "Perfectly Paranormal"), which Virginia had begun in Weston before secession and the start of hostilities.

Since the gold coins, worth a face value of $27,000 then but more than $600,000 now, were considered Confederate property and the spoils of war, McClellan decided to act on Hale's information. He ordered Colonel Erastus Tyler of the Seventh Ohio Voluntary Infantry to "confiscate all the gold in the Weston Bank, by force if necessary," and "ship it to Governor [Francis H.] Pierpont at Wheeling [the provisional capital]. Hurrah for New Virginia!"

McClellan's "New Virginia" name may not have stuck, but Colonel Tyler stuck to his orders. A fur merchant in civilian life, Tyler had visited Weston on many occasions. He and his Ohio troops marched through the night of June 29, and at first light on June 30, marched down Weston's Main Avenue with the regimental band playing "The Star-Spangled Banner," guaranteeing the wakefulness of the town's 820 residents.

The Exchange Bank was located in three rooms of a large home also occupied by the bank's manager, Robert J. McCandlish. When McCandlish heard the band and marching Union troops, he rushed downstairs, opened the front door, and found himself face-to-face with Tyler and three armed infantrymen. A Union loyalist himself, the bank official quickly complied with Tyler's demands, though he did

Taxing Situation

The sales tax is a West Virginia invention that is more unpopular today than when it first went into use on July 1, 1921.

Initially limited to banks, public utilities, and extractive industries like coal, timber, oil, and gas, the sales tax was gradually applied to virtually everything sold in the state. While West Virginia was the first state in the nation to introduce the sales tax, it certainly wasn't the last. Eight years after West Virginia took the regressive lead, Georgia followed suit. Today, only five states do not assess sales taxes.

unsuccessfully ask Tyler to leave some of the gold that was owed local laborers for their work on the hospital.

The Union regiment set up camp on the grounds of the partially built hospital and waited until a wagon from Wheeling arrived the following day to carry the gold back for deposit in the Restoration Government of Virginia's new treasury.

The home housing the Exchange Bank still stands at 137 Bank Street, and the robbery is reenacted annually during Weston's Gold Dollar Days' celebration in June.

Perfectly Paranormal
Weston

It took more than twenty years and a Civil War to complete construction of what was initially known as the Trans-Allegheny Lunatic Asylum in Weston. There was a lot to build: The blue sandstone and masonry structure may be the largest hand-cut stone building in the United States.

Today, the huge building is perhaps the nation's largest indoor ghost-hunting site, drawing thousands of visitors to Weston to search for paranormal activity in the spooky-looking, long-vacant mental ward.

Authorized by the Virginia Assembly in the early 1850s, work began on the huge structure in 1858. Work was suspended during the Civil War, and soldiers from both north and south camped on the hospital grounds at various times during the conflict (see previous entry "Government Robbery"). When West Virginia became a state in 1863, the hospital was renamed the West Virginia Hospital for the Insane, and the first patients were admitted the following year. But it took until1881 to complete the 242,000-square-foot building, which includes a 200-foot-tall clock tower.

The building was designed to promote a new concept of mental health therapy called moral treatment, in which patients were housed in spacious, well-ventilated, well-lit buildings on a parklike campus and were encouraged to work outdoors in hospital-owned gardens and farms. A farm with a large dairy component was operated on the slopes behind the building.

Problems began to arise after the hospital, built to accommodate 250 patients, came to house as many as 2,400 in the 1950s. Eventually, the new William R. Sharpe Jr. Hospital was built in Weston to replace the old West Virginia State Hospital, which closed in 1994.

Reuse plans for the huge building and surrounding property included developing it into a Civil War museum and hotel, a golf course and lodge, and a gambling casino complex. None of those concepts materialized, so the badly deteriorated hospital was put on the auction block in 2007 and sold to a Morgantown man for $1.5 million.

The former Trans-Allegheny Lunatic Asylum, once teeming with patients, now serves ghost hunters. Kenny Kemp

While other reuse plans are contemplated, the hospital is being operated as a daytime historic tourist attraction and a paranormal investigation site at night. Two-hour after dark and eight-hour overnight tours of the center are popular. The hospital has been featured in a segment of the Sci-Fi Channel's *Ghost Hunters* series.

For details, visit www.trans-alleghenylunaticasylum.com, or call (304) 269-5070.

Stogies' Starting Place
Wheeling

In 1840 Wheeling, at the western end of the National Road (also known as the Cumberland Road, currently US 40) leading from Chesapeake Bay, was a major supply center and jumping-off point for westbound settlers and teamsters, who often arrived in town in canvas-covered Conestoga wagons.

This old Wheeling scene shows the Marsh-Wheeling cigar factory at center. West Virginia State Archives

Match This

The world's biggest shipment of stick matches—210 million in all—was shipped from Wheeling to Memphis on August 26, 1933. It took twenty railcars to handle the West Virginia–made matches.

At about that time, a Wheeling cigar maker named Miflin Marsh began producing a long, thin cigar that soon became popular with the wagon drivers, as well as the steamboat passengers and crew who docked at the town's Ohio River wharves. The smoke became known as a "stogie," a shortened nickname for the Conestoga wagon.

Marsh initially made the stogies in his home and sold them from a market basket he carried over his arm. But the demand grew so rapidly, he built a factory in downtown Wheeling to mass-produce the slender cigar. The Marsh Wheeling factory remained in operation until 2001, when an Indiana firm bought the cigar maker. At the time of its closure, it was the oldest cigar company in the nation.

Crystal Bowl Gazing

Wheeling

When Wheeling glassmaker Michael Sweeney died in 1875, a granite monument housing the world's largest cut lead crystal punch bowl was placed atop his grave.

It wasn't because Sweeney was fond of punch.

The crystal piece was one of three multiple-sectioned cut glass punch bowls, or float bowls, as they were also known, created by Sweeney and his brothers in their Wheeling shop in the 1840s. The huge pieces were made for display on the industrial fair circuit, including London's Crystal Palace exposition. But a fire in the early 1850s

Chewish Culture

In the 1870s officials at the Bloch Brothers Tobacco Company came up with a way of recycling the trimmings from the cigars they produced in their Wheeling factory that was nothing to spit at: They placed the scrap tobacco in paper bags and sold it as West Virginia Mail Pouch Tobacco, later shortened to Mail Pouch. Initially, the bagged tobacco was marketed to both smokers and chewers, but within a few years, the emphasis shifted from inhaling to expectorating.

A barn near Dunlow carries an advertising message viewers can sink their teeth into. Steve Shaluta

In one of the nation's first and most imaginative interstate out-door advertising campaigns, the Bloch Brothers promoted their product in a manner that targeted their demographic group—rural men—by painting barns with the Mail Pouch logo and the slogan "Treat Yourself to the Best." The campaign, launched in 1890, spread to nine Appalachian and Midwest states, plus Washington, Oregon, and California. Cooperating barn owners got a free coat of paint with periodic touch-ups and collected a small cash fee plus a quantity of Mail Pouch products. More than 4,000 barns and outbuildings were painted by roving crews hired by the Bloch Brothers. In the 1960s the barn-painting campaign began to sput-ter due to new scenic highway laws restricting outdoor advertising and a switch to television and radio advertising in response to a declining rural customer base.

In 1974 Mail Pouch barns were designated National Historic Land-marks, generating a new wave of touch-up work, but by the end of 1992, no more barns were painted. Interest in the folksy com-mercial artwork remains strong enough to have created a national organization of Mail Pouch Barnstormers, who photograph remain-ing barns, interview former barn painters, and keep tabs on the restoration and demolition of Mail Pouch–adorned structures. About 200 West Virginia barns and outbuildings received the Mail Pouch treatment during the course of the advertising campaign.

★ ★

destroyed the Sweeneys' Wheeling glassworks and preempted show-ing the huge pieces abroad.

Michael Sweeney died in 1875, and the huge crystal bowl perched atop his grave—the sole remaining large crystal punch bowl—was removed from the monument in 1949 over fears that it would be damaged or destroyed if left in the cemetery. It is now displayed in the Oglebay Institute Glass Museum.

The Sweeney Punch Bowl is nearly 5 feet tall, weighs 225 pounds, and is the largest piece of cut lead crystal ever made. It also packs

Mr. Motivation
Where did Jack Canfield, cocre-ator of the popular *Chicken Soup for the Soul* series, get the recipe for his series of uplifting best sellers?

It could have been Wheeling, where he grew up during the 1950s.

Canfield wrote that his father worked in a Wheeling floral shop, earn-ing no more than $8,000 a year, while his mother was a stay-at-home alcoholic. Young Canfield worked as a swimming pool lifeguard and in the same flower shop as his dad.

"Nobody handed me anything on a silver platter," Canfield wrote. "I worked during the summers to make ends meet." He earned a scholar-ship to Linsly Institute, a private boarding school in Wheeling, where he apparently studied hard enough to be accepted at Harvard. There, he struggled to meet his expenses, perfecting not chicken soup, but something he called his Twenty-one-Cent Dinner, which consisted of a ten-cent can of tomato paste, a dash of garlic, and an eleven-cent bag of spaghetti noodles.

a lot of punch—16 gallons' worth, to be precise. The museum is located at 1330 National Road, Wheeling. For more information, call (304) 242-7272.

Getting Nailed in Wheeling
Wheeling

If it worked okay 150 years ago, why change it?

That seems to be part of the operational philosophy at the LaBelle Iron Works factory in Wheeling, where cut nails used in masonry, carpentry, and historic restoration projects have been manufactured since 1852.

The largest and last-remaining cut nail factory in the world, the LaBelle plant was once one of several nail factories operating in Wheeling. Its nail-making machines were initially powered by steam produced from coal mined in the hillside behind the plant but are now driven by electric motors.

The city's nail output once accounted for more than 30 percent of the nation's nail production. The industry also inspired the name of the city's East Coast Hockey League team, the Wheeling Nailers.

The LaBelle Iron Works factory occasionally arranges tours of its South Wheeling works. For information, call (304) 232-1355, or visit www.wheeling-labelle.com.

A Bridge Too Fair
Wheeling

While most of the traffic it now carries is destined for a racetrack and casino on Wheeling Island, the Wheeling Suspension Bridge was once the nation's gateway for westward expansion as well as the world's largest suspension span.

Completed in 1849, the bridge was the first in the nation to cross the Ohio River. It carried horse- and oxen-powered traffic from the National Road, then the nation's main east–west highway, into the

Legendary Leap

Surrounded by Indians while trying to reach besieged Fort Henry with militia reinforcements on September 1, 1777, Major Samuel McColloch turned his horse in the only direction not blocked by members of the ambushing war party and galloped toward the edge of a bluff.

The details about what happened next vary from account to account, but one fact is constant: McColloch and his horse survived a jaw-dropping plunge into Wheeling Creek. According to varying accounts of the feat, McColloch and his horse plummeted as far as 400 feet, and as few as 150 feet, off either a sheer precipice or a steep slope, suffering no injuries more severe than scratches and bruises.

McColloch returned to the Wheeling fort the following day with a force of forty militiamen, but by that time, the Indians had broken off the siege. A granite monument along US 40 near the site of the incident recounts the legend and features a bas relief image of a mounted, musket-waving McColloch plunging off the precipice.

A timeworn highway marker shows a musket-waving Samuel McColloch leaping off a cliff atop his steed.

Ohio country and beyond. It is the oldest suspension highway bridge still in use.

Designed by Charles Ellet Jr., the Wheeling bridge's main span stretches 1,010 feet from the downtown Wheeling shore across the main channel of the Ohio River, making it the longest bridge of its kind in the world at the time of its completion.

Financed through the sale of stock, the bridge charged tolls in its early years to recover the investment. In 1849 it cost a horse and rider 10 cents to cross the span, while the fee was 2 cents for each hog or sheep herded across the river.

Today, most Wheeling area traffic crosses the Ohio over the I-70 or I-470 bridges. The old suspension bridge still serves hundreds of residents of Wheeling Island and thousands of patrons of the Wheeling Island Hotel, Casino, and Racetrack. At the time of its opening, Ellet said the bridge was capable of resisting 297 tons, a weight equal to "32 heavy-laden road wagons, 192 horses, and 500 people." Its weight limit is now 4,000 pounds per vehicle. The eastern end of the bridge is located at the corner of Main Street and Tenth Street in downtown Wheeling.

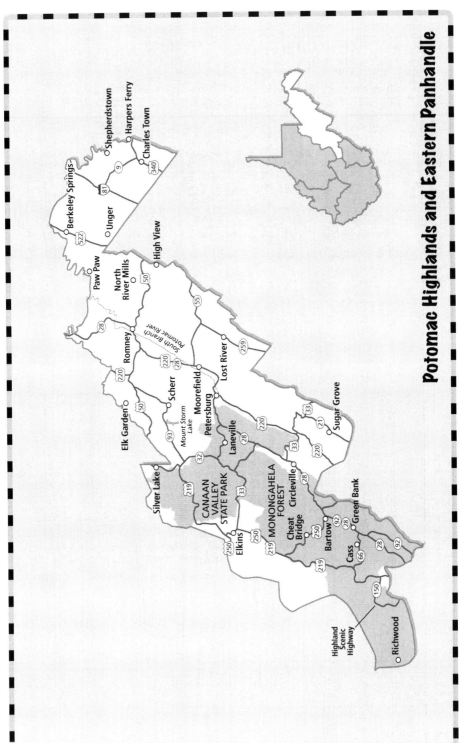

Potomac Highlands and Eastern Panhandle

5

Potomac Highlands and Eastern Panhandle

With terrain that often looks more Canadian than Appalachian, West Virginia's Potomac Highlands surprise many visitors. In this part of the state, much of the land above 3,500 feet—and there's a lot of it—is covered by a nearly unbroken evergreen forest of red spruce and occasional stands of balsam fir. Streams are filled with trout instead of bass, and northland critters like bobcats, fishers, and snowshoe hares roam the woods. It's a mountain-biking mecca and a backpacking paradise for eastern urbanites eager to lose themselves in the state's million acres of national forest land, where it's possible to drive 30 miles along the Highland Scenic Highway and not see a single house, power line, or cell phone tower.

To the east the mountains begin to descend, and the valleys start to extend as the terrain gradually gets less extreme. Harpers Ferry, the state's easternmost point, is also its lowest, with an elevation of only 247 feet. The fastest growing part of what is now West Virginia in the mid-1700s, the Eastern Panhandle continues to be the state's hot spot for new development due to its close proximity to Washington and Baltimore. Conflicts between preservationists and developers are many, but the blend of old and new adds to the vibrancy of the area, creating an abundance of curiosities. Here are a few.

Holding the Highest Ground

Bartow

Built in the summer of 1861 in an open meadow at an elevation of 4,400 feet, Camp Allegheny—the highest Civil War fortress east of the Mississippi—dealt its Confederate garrison enough bad weather and disease to make fighting off a Yankee attack almost preferable.

The mountaintop position, held by poorly supplied troops from Georgia and Virginia, included an enclosed pit and parapet fortress, cabins, fortified artillery emplacements, and trenches. Camp Allegheny

At 4,400 feet, Camp Allegheny was the highest—and coldest—Civil War fort east of the Mississippi.

overlooked the pass through which the Staunton–Parkersburg Turnpike traversed a high ridge in the Allegheny Mountains before descending into the Greenbrier River Valley.

Exposed to the elements and a magnet for precipitation, the alpine encampment experienced a snowfall in August 1861. The freak winter storm gave the 1,200 southern troops a taste of the cold, wet weather they would endure before being attacked by a Union force of about 1,900 men on December 12. On that day a simultaneous two-pronged attack had been planned by the federal troops, but one of the prongs encountered a Confederate picket line and was forced to start the raid prematurely.

The Confederate garrison successfully fought off the larger Union force, and each side lost 20 killed and about 120 wounded or missing. During the remainder of the winter, measles, pneumonia, and other diseases swept through the camp, claiming nearly as many victims as the Union troops.

"Between the measles and the worst climate ever seen, I am still dragging out a kind of miserable existence, unable to do military duty or anything else," George P. Morgan, an infantryman in the Thirty-first Virginia Regiment, wrote in his diary. "Here on top of the Allegheny Mountain it rains in torrents nearly every day, and when not raining, we can't see 50 yards."

The earth and rock walls of the fort, abandoned in April 1862, can still be plainly seen in the middle of an open sheep pasture on private land. The U.S. Forest Service manages property bordering the fort, including a section where foundation and fireplace stones for at least thirty-five Confederate cabins can be found. A small picnic area on the Forest Service land includes a series of interpretive signs that point out the main features of the encampment and tell the story of the Union attack.

From US 219 at Bartow, Camp Allegheny can be reached by following State Secondary Route 3, a moderately well-maintained dirt road, 9 miles to the top of Buffalo Mountain, along the path of the old Staunton–Parkersburg Turnpike. Look for gun pits, trenches, and earthen walls in the pasture at the summit, then watch for a Forest Service overlook/picnic area.

Washington Soaked Here?
Berkeley Springs

A sign above a small rectangular pool lined with cut rock at the base of Warm Springs Ridge in Berkeley Springs State Park identifies the site as George Washington's bathtub.

But did the famed Revolutionary War general actually soak his presidential privates in the craggy outdoor tub?

While there is little doubt that Washington did take the waters at Berkeley Springs during repeated summer visits to the Morgan County town, he didn't use the rocky, rectangular receptacle, since it is a relatively modern reconstruction of the primitive facilities used by early bathers. The rock tub was first identified as George Washington's bathtub in 1930.

Washington first visited the springs, which burst out of the ground at a rate of 2,000 gallons per minute at a temperature of 74.3 degrees Fahrenheit, on March 18, 1748. At the time, he was a sixteen-year-old member of a survey crew. He returned many times over the years, bought two lots in the town in 1777, and commissioned James Rumsey, who later invented a working version of the steamboat twenty years before Robert Fulton, to build a vacation home there.

Washington was not the only early American mover and shaker to buy property in the spa town. Four signers of the Constitution and three men who signed the Declaration of Independence bought land here in the late 1700s, along with five Revolutionary War generals and seven members of the Continental Congress.

The town, officially known as Bath but doing business as Berkeley Springs, has kept in touch with its spa-town roots. It has three times as many licensed massage therapists as lawyers and four spas with programs and amenities beyond what the state park offers. Each year, the people of Berkeley Springs pay tribute to their most famous summer guest by holding the annual George Washington's Bathtub Celebration—a program of history-related activities and retail sales. The festival takes place on the weekend closest to March 18—the date in 1748 when Washington first visited the springs.

Berkeley Springs State Park is the only unit of the state park system where massage therapists are on the payroll. The park has a Roman bathhouse with 750-gallon individual pools, where visitors presoak before receiving Swedish-style rubdowns.

Call (304) 258-2711, or visit www.berkeleyspringssp.com.

A Man's Castle Is His Home
Berkeley Springs

One way to convince a woman nearly thirty years your junior to marry you is to promise you will build her a castle if she agrees. At least that's the approach that worked for Samuel Taylor Suit, a wealthy businessman and former Maryland state senator, who met and fell in love with Rosa Pelham, the seventeen-year-old daughter of an Alabama congressman, while vacationing in the Morgan County spa town of Berkeley Springs in the 1880s.

Suit, who founded a distillery in Louisville, had a seat on the New York Stock Exchange, and married and divorced the daughter of an insurance magnate before meeting Pelham, began work on the castle in 1885, on a slope of Warm Springs Ridge overlooking Berkeley Springs. German stonemasons used hand-cut sandstone to build the English-Norman-style castle. It took six years to complete, and Suit did not live long enough to see it. His wife completed the thirteen-room mini-palace, complete with a ballroom, dungeon, and turrets, and hosted numerous parties for her Washington, D.C., friends.

Rosa Pelham Suit lived large until her funds ran out, forcing the castle to go on the auction block in 1914, when she moved into a small house and raised chickens before moving to Idaho with a son.

Since then, the castle has been used as a summer camp for boys and a public museum. It is now in private ownership and has been restored but is no longer open for tours. It is open for weddings, fund-raisers, and corporate events.

For a close look at the castle, drive or walk up WV 9 from downtown Berkeley Springs.

Down on the Snow Farm

Canaan Valley

West Virginia may not be a likely locale for an upcoming Winter Olympics, Senator Robert C. Byrd's influence notwithstanding. But the state does have a lot more to offer, in terms of alpine and Nordic sports, than out-of-state snow buffs might suspect.

More than 500,000 people a year buy lift tickets to ski and snowboard at the state's four ski resorts—Snowshoe Mountain, Winterplace, Timberline, and Canaan Valley Resort State Park, where vertical drops of up to 1,500 feet can be found, along with trails in the 2-mile range. While winter snowfalls totaling 150 inches or more are common, miles of water pipe and large arsenals of state-of-the-art snowmaking equipment are what keep the snow resorts profitable and the skiers and riders happy south of the Mason–Dixon line.

But at White Grass, the state's most popular cross-country ski area, snow management is a low-tech procedure that the resort's operator, Chip Chase, has nudged toward perfection since setting up shop in Canaan Valley in 1979.

It starts just before the snow flies, by removing every rock, stick, and limb from every trail, allowing them to open with only a few inches of snow. Along the pastures surrounding the shedlike White Grass lodge, even the cowpies have to be pulverized, since "they're just like a rock when you hit 'em with your skis," according to Chase.

Most of the trail-clearing work is done by volunteers who donate their labor for free trail passes.

A Nordic skier takes a telemark turn at White Grass, the busiest Nordic resort south of the Mason–Dixon line.

Miles of lightweight webbed plastic fences are spread across the open glades to capture wind-blown drifting snow. Once snow starts to drift over the fences, "we move them like fishermen move their nets, to catch as much snow as possible," Chase explains.

Once fence-high thicknesses of snow are captured, they are rolled and groomed with snowmobile-towed gear or the resort's snow-grooming machine. Finally, a mechanical track setter stamps a perfect Nordic ski track into the groomed trail.

White Grass maintains 50 kilometers (about 31 miles) of groomed trails, many of them extending into the adjacent Canaan Valley National Wildlife Refuge under a special-use agreement. Elevations range from 3,200 feet near the White Grass lodge to 4,400 feet atop Cabin Mountain.

A restaurant in the weather-beaten but cozy lodge at White Grass features hearty natural foods and vegetarian fare and is popular with skiers and nonskiers alike. Dinner reservations are mandatory.

White Grass is located within a snowball's throw of the slope where the ski tracks were made in Canaan Valley. In the early 1950s members of the Washington, D.C., Ski Club began exploring the slopes south of Pennsylvania for signs of snow following an unusually snow-deficient winter. A member of the club who was a pilot spotted drifts of snow in the steep, shady south end of the valley from the air and mentioned the site to other club members, who followed up with a road trip.

The ski club rented a hillside pasture from a Canaan Valley farmer and by the mid-1950s were operating two rope tows there. In 1959 Bob and Anita Barton began operations on a neighboring slope, offering snowmaking, four rope tows, and a base lodge. It is there that Chase and his wife, Laurie Little, now operate White Grass.

For information on West Virginia skiing and snowboarding, visit www.wvwintersports.com, or call the Division of Tourism at (800) CALL-WVA. For more on White Grass, visit www.whitegrass.com, or call (304) 866-4114.

Company Town for Rent

Cass

Have the urge to live like a timber baron? At Cass Scenic Railroad State Park, you can rent an entire company town and lord over it for as long as your credit card limit allows.

I know you're not most people, but most people just rent one of the former company town's restored and refurbished employee cottages for use as a headquarters in exploring the surrounding mountains aboard the steam-powered Cass Scenic Railroad. But the entire town—or large parts of it—is available to rent for family reunions and company retreats.

Cass Scenic Railroad State Park encompasses much of the old saw-mill town of Cass, where the now-defunct West Virginia Pulp & Paper Company built dozens of homes for use by company employees and their families. Twenty of the homes have been restored by the state park and are available for rent year-round.

The two-story wood frame homes date to the early 1900s, when Cass was a rough-and-tumble logging and lumber boom town as the surrounding forest and its giant trees were cut and processed for the first time. They are fully furnished, kitchen equipped, and capable of housing six to ten people each. A newly refurbished five-bedroom manager's house can sleep up to sixteen.

From the former company houses, it's a short walk down the hill to the former company store, which now serves as a grocery/cafe/

Former mill town housing now shelters tourists.

souvenir stand for the Cass Scenic Railroad. The railroad station fronts the Greenbrier River, where anglers can stalk trout and others can float on inner tubes through pools and mild rapids. Bicyclists can roll onto the Greenbrier River Trail and ride the former railbed around the next bend in the river, or 78 miles to the outskirts of Lewisburg. Snowshoe Mountain Resort, the state's largest ski area, is a fifteen-minute drive away.

For more information, call (304) 456-4300 or (800) CALL-WVA, or visit www.cassrailroad.com.

Footloose Cabooses
Cass

If you like your vacations peaceful, quiet, close to nature, and far from the maddening crowd—without having to backpack or ride a horse—why not let the state of West Virginia run you out of town on a rail?

In addition to operating scenic excursion train rides to 4,800-foot-high Bald Knob on Cheat Mountain, Cass Scenic Railroad State Park offers backcountry caboose rentals at remote sidings off the tourist train's main line.

One of the most remote rental railcars is Caboose 311, which is generally stationed at Bald Knob, along a strip of state-owned railroad right-of-way in the midst of a vast tract of backcountry in the Monongahela National Forest. The 1940-vintage caboose is supplied with drinking water, coal for a railcar's coal stove, a propane refrigerator/freezer, a dinette for six, an array of bunk beds, and a day bed. Those staying in the caboose must bring their own sleeping bags, food, cooking and dining utensils, camping lights, and fuel. A camp stove and fuel are also recommended, since the coal stove is tricky to cook on.

Caboose campers reach the mountaintop siding by riding the steam-powered Cass Scenic Railroad Bald Knob train and carrying their gear a short distance to the siding. Sweeping views of the Greenbrier River Valley and the Allegheny ridges along the Virginia–West Virginia

Buccaneer of the Ohio

The life of crime for one of America's most infamous river pirates began in West Virginia, where, according to at least one historic account, he cut his teeth by stealing horses in the Eastern Panhandle, then moved on to stealing government supplies in the Northern Panhandle.

According to other accounts, Samuel Mason was a law-abiding citizen and Revolutionary War hero while in what is now West Virginia before mysteriously assuming the life of a murderous criminal after moving out of state.

All accounts agree that Mason was born in Norfolk, Virginia, and grew up in the Charles Town area before moving to Wheeling in about 1773. In January 1777 he was appointed a captain in the Virginia militia and charged with keeping attacks by British-supplied Native Americans at bay in the upper Ohio River Valley. In September 1777 he was wounded and most of the men in his company killed in an Indian ambush near Wheeling's Fort Henry. After the war he relocated to southwestern Pennsylvania, where he ran up an impressive amount of debt, and fled to eastern Tennessee, where he took up robbery, larceny, and murder before deciding that the future was in river piracy.

Along the banks of the Ohio near present-day Henderson, Kentucky, Mason and his crew attacked flatboats carrying merchandise or families of settlers downriver. After a few years residents of the area had their fill of Mason and his gang. They formed a posse and drove the outlaws out of town. They eventually came to roost on a stretch of the lower Ohio in Illinois where a large cave overlooks an expanse of the river. At Cave-in-Rock, Mason operated a bar and brothel and continued to rob and murder passing travelers.

The 1955 Walt Disney movie *Davy Crockett and the River Pirates* was loosely based on Mason's life of crime in the Cave-in-Rock area. The cave and a similar river pirate were also included in the 1962 epic *How the West Was Won*.

Pushed out of southern Illinois as a law enforcement system began to develop there, Mason set up shop along the Spanish-controlled lower Mississippi, plundering river traffic almost at will until 1803, when the territorial governor offered a $500 reward for his capture. He was beheaded by members of his own gang. They, in turn, were arrested and hanged when they attempted to claim their reward.

border can be seen to the east, while an unbroken expanse of alpine wilderness stretches toward the western horizon.

The nearby West Virginia Central Railroad also offers caboose camping from its hub in the town of Durbin. Campers ride to their

A Life of Slime

The black bear may be West Virginia's official state mammal and the timber rattler the official state reptile, but no woodland critter displays more home-state loyalty than the smaller, slimier Cheat Mountain salamander. Its entire world population never ventures outside the borders of five West Virginia counties.

First discovered in 1935 on a promontory of Cheat Mountain, the 4-inch-long salamander has a black or dark brown back flecked with specks of gold or silver. Its primary habitat is red spruce forests, particularly those occurring at elevations. Since most of the state's high-altitude spruce stands were clear-cut in the 1920s, the salamanders have learned to adapt in moist, shady mixed hardwood forests at slightly lower elevations.

Although the salamanders are on the federal endangered species list, most of their habitat lies either in the Monongahela National Forest or the Canaan Valley National Wildlife Refuge, making it easier for federal wildlife biologists to manage their recovery. In recent years their numbers seem to have stabilized.

The moisture-loving salamanders, which can live twenty years or more, don't live to travel. Not only have they not ventured outside West Virginia since the last ice age, they seldom leave a 48-square-foot section of territory they stake out upon reaching sexual maturity.

remote siding along the Greenbrier River in one of two refurbished original Wabash Railroad cabooses, each equipped with refrigerators, ranges, heaters, linens, towels, utensils, showers, and restrooms. The cabooses are transported to and from the overnight siding, which is also surrounded by the Monongahela National Forest, by the steam-powered *Durbin Rocket* excursion train.

For more information about caboose camping with the Cass Scenic Railroad, call (800) CALL-WVA, or (304) 456-4300, or visit www.cassrail road.com. To learn more about caboose camping via the *Durbin Rocket,* call (877) 686-7245 or (304) 636-9477, or visit www.mountainrail.com.

RFD One
Charles Town

Postmaster General William Wilson's West Virginia roots were show-ing when he established the nation's first Rural Free Delivery mail sys-tem on October 1, 1896.

Wilson selected his native Jefferson County as the official test-ing ground for a system of free mail delivery to farmers and others who live far from larger communities served by letter carriers. Wilson assigned three horseback-riding RFD carriers to the Charles Town area, his former hometown, and one carrier each to Halltown and Uvilla.

The experiment was a success. Within five years, there were 2,551 RFD routes providing mail service to nearly two million people.

Roughing It with Henry Ford
Cheat

A remote lodge that once attracted the quartet of the automaker Henry Ford, the inventor Thomas Edison, the tire magnate Harvey Firestone, and the naturalist John Burroughs for a week of "roughing it" in the wilds of Cheat Mountain is still available to outdoor-loving guests.

Built in 1887 as the headquarters for a large hunting and fish-ing preserve, the Cheat Mountain Club is perched on a bank of the

Shavers Fork River, a scenic trout stream, and surrounded by the Monongahela National Forest, miles from the nearest town. As Edison wrote in the club's guest register, it is "a beautiful spot."

Ford, Edison, Firestone, and Burroughs stayed at the CMC in 1918, en route to an auto tour of the Smoky Mountains. The "Four Vagabonds," as they called themselves, took similar vehicular-supported trips throughout the early 1920s, pioneering the concept of car camping—though on a fairly grand scale.

En route to their stay at the CMC, the Four Vagabonds were briefly accompanied by President Warren G. Harding when the Lincoln touring car in which they were riding got stuck in the mud along a West Virginia back road on a rainy day.

According to a *Detroit News* account of the incident, Ford's chauffeur went for help and returned with a nearby farmer and a Model T Ford. After the farmer pulled the Lincoln from the mudhole, Ford reportedly said, "I guess you don't know me, but I'm Henry Ford. I made the car you're driving." Firestone quickly identified himself as "the man who made those tires," pointing to the farmer's vehicle. Then he introduced the remaining campers as "the man who invented the electric light and the president of the United States." While Burroughs introduced himself, he told the farmer, "I guess you don't know me, either," as he shook the West Virginian's hand.

"No," the farmer replied. "But if you're the same kind of liar as these other darned fools, I wouldn't be surprised if you said you was Santa Claus."

Fly-fishing, mountain biking, hiking, cross-country skiing, and lounging in front of the club's large fireplace are among the most popular activities of CMC guests in the twenty-first century. The ten-bedroom lodge is rented as a complete inn, rather than room by room.

For details, visit www.cheatmountainclub.com, or call (304) 456-4627.

Cliff Hanging
Circleville

For anyone who has ever yearned to scale a series of sheer cliffs rising several hundred feet without having to go through the time and effort of actually learning how to climb—and live to tell about it—Nelson Rocks Preserve near Riverton is the place to be.

Nelson Rocks is the home of the nation's second via ferrata, a climbing route with a safety system permanently installed, allowing nonclimbers to experience adrenalin-enhancing vertical climbs along the "iron road," as *via ferrata* translates from the Italian. Climbers wear a harness attached to their waists and legs, which in turn is connected to a pair of carabiners, or climbing clips. As climbers move up the via ferrata route, they clip the carabiners onto a fixed cable, keeping them connected to firmly anchored hardware at all times—if they don't forget to clip in.

In addition to a series of vertical pitches, via ferrata climbers cross a 200-foot-long suspension footbridge, which dangles 150 feet above a jagged boulder field and resembles a scene in an *Indiana Jones* movie. The bridge connects two "fins" of quartzite cliffs used on the climbing route.

Thousands of people have climbed the via ferrata since it opened in 2002. If used properly, the fixed system prevents climbers from falling farther than their lowest clip-in point, but injuries can occur if climbers lose their footing and swing into the cliff face.

For those interested in spectacular views without having to go completely vertical to attain them, Nelson Rocks' trail system takes hikers to the tops of the fins for great views of the Allegheny Highlands, Germany Valley, and people scaling the cliffs below.

Via ferrata climbs are booked by appointment only by calling Nelson Rocks Preserve at (304) 567-3169. All safety gear is provided as part of the via ferrata climbing fee. Nelson Rocks Preserve is located 11 miles south of Seneca Rocks, about ½ mile off WV 28. Visit www.nelsonrocks.org for more information.

A Monumental Dunk

Elkins

An audience of only about one hundred people was on hand at the Randolph County Armory on December 21, 1984, when Georgann Wells became the first woman in history to make a slam dunk in an official NCAA collegiate game.

Wells, a 6-foot, 7-inch center for West Virginia University, made the record-setting dunk, using a regulation-size "men's" basketball during a 110–82 win over the University of Charleston, played during the annual Mountaineer Christmas Classic tournament.

Reaction to her scoring the dunk from her teammates was so loud and prolonged that the team drew a technical foul. In addition to scoring the historic slam, Wells racked up 1,484 points and pulled down 1,075 rebounds in her four-year career with the Mountaineers. It took ten years for another woman to duplicate Wells's dunking feat, and that slam involved an intermediate-size "women's" basketball.

University of Charleston's coach Bud Francis made the only video recording of the game but refused to release it to WVU or the media. A Charleston lawyer, Ford Francis, found the tape in 2009, when a *Wall Street Journal* reporter, preparing a story on the twenty-fifth anniversary of the feat, asked him to look through his late father's files for the historic film.

13,000 Miles of Quiet

Green Bank

It's not just a series of rugged, 4,000-foot-high mountain ranges and an absence of population centers that make it hard to yack on the cell phone or catch the latest scores on the radio while traveling through a 13,000-square-mile expanse of mostly U.S. Forest Service land along the West Virginia–Virginia border.

If you're anywhere along a 120-mile-long, 115-mile wide swath of land stretching from Parsons in the north to White Sulphur Springs in

Take Your Best Shot

West Virginia is fairly well known as a place where people can learn to stalk and kill deer, turkey, and bear. But Storm Mountain Training Center near Elk Garden takes the state's hunting tradition a step further. It may be the only place in the nation offering civilians intensive training in how to stalk and kill people.

Storm Mountain's Sniper School, taught by experts with lengthy military and law enforcement experience, is designed to provide students with "the technical skills and operational procedures necessary to deliver precision rifle fire from concealed positions onto selected targets."

The program caters mainly to military and law enforcement groups. But civilians willing to fork out $1,100 for the five-day course are also invited to learn how to "achieve first-round hits from a cold barrel into high value targets," according to the course description on Storm Mountain's Web site.

Armchair snipers need not apply. Sniper School participants must have previously passed Storm Mountain's Long Range Rifle I course and be able to do forty push-ups in two minutes and run 1.5 miles in less than fourteen minutes.

Storm Mountain's 250-acre campus offers plenty of room for concealment and stalking exercises for its Sniper School, as well as its programs in handgun and long rifle skills, urban warfare, and the protection of high-risk personnel. It's highly recommended by *S.W.A.T.* magazine.

For details, visit www.stormmountain.com, or call (304) 446-5526.

the south, you're in the National Radio Quiet Zone, a place where Big Brother may not be watching, but is definitely listening.

Set aside in 1958 by the Federal Communications Commission as sort of an electromagnetic pollution-free wilderness area, the NRQZ was created to accommodate two new government facilities that needed an absence of radio interference in order to operate. One is the National Radio Astronomy Observatory at Green Bank, which captures and analyzes extremely weak radio signals from deep space. The other is the Navy Information Operations Command base at Sugar Grove, which has been linked to the National Security Agency's electronic intelligence-gathering arm.

While high-powered transmitters are forbidden, the zone is not completely radio free. All major transmitters within the zone must coordinate their operations with NRQZ staffers, who maintain a small office at the Green Bank observatory. Cell phone base stations are not allowed within close proximity to either Green Bank or Sugar Grove and are few and far between on the fringes of the zone. The few radio stations operating within the zone, such as Allegheny Public Radio in Frost, must point their antennas away from the two facilities and run on reduced power. Wireless modems and cordless phones are regulated within a 10-mile radius of Green Bank, where power lines must be buried 4 feet below ground to prevent incidental electromagnetic interference.

Personnel from the NRQZ routinely patrol their 13,000-square-mile domain to track down sources of research-damaging interference, which have ranged from transmissions from a Russian satellite to faulty garage door openers.

One of the most vexing sources of broadband interference to radio telescope operations at Green Bank was traced to a site 1 mile east of the observatory. There, an elderly couple had placed a worn-out electric heating pad with cracked wiring outside their mobile home for their dog to sleep on. NRQZ staffers replaced the old dog warmer with a new one.

At NRAO Green Bank, workers ride bikes or drive diesel-powered—and sparkplug-free—vehicles to work stations near the facility's parabolic dish antennas. All microwave ovens within the office complex and visitor center are equipped with extra shielding. A fleet of aging, diesel-powered (no sparkplugs) Checker taxicabs is available for visiting scientists and VIPs. Visitors touring the observatory must leave digital cameras in their cars.

The National Radio Quiet Zone maintains an office at NRAO Green Bank. For more information, visit www.gb.nrao.edu/nrqz.

Searching for ET
Green Bank

The Deer Creek Valley of Pocahontas County is known locally for its prime trout fishing, scenic pastureland, and namesake population of whitetails that gather in herds large enough to make drivers on WV 28 pull over and gawk. But in 1960 the remote valley was the setting for a quest that went far beyond deer, trout, and mountain scenery: the world's first scientific search for intelligent life in the universe.

Frank Drake, who earned his doctorate in astronomy from Harvard the year before, had recently been assigned as an astronomer at the new National Radio Astronomy Observatory at Green Bank, in the heart of the Deer Creek Valley, where an 85-foot radio telescope had just been installed. Since childhood, Drake had been curious about the possibility of other civilizations existing elsewhere in the universe. He calculated that if other worlds could send radio signals of a strength equal to those sent on Earth, the new Green Bank scope was capable of detecting them, if they originated within ten light years of Earth.

Drake and other scientists at Green Bank met regularly for lunch at a greasy spoon cafe they jokingly called "Pierre's," about 5 miles away from the observatory. During one such session in the winter of 1959, Drake posed the idea of pointing the new radio telescope at some nearby stars in hopes of picking up signals produced by

The Green Bank telescope searches for pulsars and the deep-space building blocks of stars.

advanced life forms. His colleagues liked the idea, although they were a bit leery of generating unwanted publicity over searching for what they would later call LGM—little green men.

The 85-foot telescope was modified with about $2,000 worth of special equipment, including an experimental parametric amplifier in the dish and a loudspeaker in the control room to augment a chart recorder.

On April 8, 1960, Project Ozma, named for Princess Ozma of Oz from the L. Frank Baum book, began. The first SETI (Search for Extra-terrestrial Intelligence) probe involved observations of Earth's two closest sunlike stars, Tau Ceti and Epsilon Eridani. Observations taken around Tau Ceti revealed nothing unexpected, so the telescope was pointed at Epsilon Eridani. After taking a few minutes of uneventful observations, the chart recorder needle began swinging wildly back and forth, and bursts of static could be heard pulsing from the speaker at eight beats per second.

"We all looked at each other wide-eyed," Drake said in a 1981 interview. "Could it be this easy?"

The signal disappeared but returned ten days later. While the astronomers were excited at first, they soon realized that the pulsing noise was just as loud coming from a simple terrestrial antenna strung through the window as it was from the huge parabolic receiver in the pasture before them. They concluded that the noise came from an airplane, most likely a military aircraft practicing electronic warfare techniques.

After a two-month search involving 200 hours of observations searching 7,200 channels, the world's first SETI search ended. While no LGM were detected, the search technique became a model for extraterrestrial intelligence scans being conducted today by the non-profit SETI Institute in Mountain View, California. And these days, scientists don't have to travel to "Pierre's" to hash out their research goals. The observatory's new visitor-friendly Science Center includes the Starlight Cafe, open to both National Radio Astronomy Observatory employees and the public.

The 85-foot radio telescope used in the historic 1960 search remains in use today as a component of the NRAO's Green Bank interferometer, a three-telescope array used to track promising gamma ray and x-ray burst sources for NASA's High Energy Astrophysics program.

The star of the star-searching hardware now in use at the remote observatory is the Green Bank telescope, which at 17 million pounds and 485 feet tall may be the largest moving structure on Earth. The telescope rolls along a circular rail and can tilt and flex its two-acre collection surface. The GBT is involved mainly in the study of pulsars and in the detection of deep-space atoms and molecules that provide clues about the formation of stars.

The GBT's official name, the Robert C. Byrd Green Bank Telescope, reflects its star power in the realm of down-home politics.

From Memorial Day through Labor Day, NRAO Green Bank is open daily for free guided tours, which depart hourly from 9:00 a.m. to 6:00 p.m. A new Science Center museum uses a number of hands-on exhibits to explain the concept of radio astronomy and trace its history. Call (304) 456-2150, or visit www.gb.nrao.edu for details.

Sweetest Surrender

Harpers Ferry

Harpers Ferry is probably best known as the site where the abolitionist John Brown and his Provisional Army of the United States seized the federal arsenal and armory in 1859 in an ill-fated attempt to equip an armed uprising of slaves.

But three years later West Virginia's easternmost town was also the scene of the largest surrender in U.S. military history, an unwanted record that stood until 1942, when American forces in the Philippines capitulated to the Japanese in the opening months of World War II.

In September 1862, 14,000 Union soldiers occupied Harpers Ferry and a patch of high ground atop nearby Bolivar Heights, as Confederate general Robert E. Lee crossed the Potomac River 15 miles away and entered Maryland to begin his Antietam campaign. On September 13, Lee sent three columns back to Harpers Ferry to neutralize the large Union garrison. A column led by Major General Thomas "Stonewall" Jackson cornered the federal positions atop Bolivar Heights, while Major General A. P. Hill's column took possession of a nearby unoccupied farm and lugged five artillery batteries up a ravine to the high ground during the night. Meanwhile, Brigadier General John Walker and his 2,000 Confederates captured an expanse of unoccupied ridgeline at nearby Loudon Heights.

Confederate artillery atop this bluff convinced nearly 12,500 Union troops to lay down their arms.

With the high ground overlooking Harpers Ferry in their control, the Confederates fired their artillery pieces at will on the Union troops below, demoralizing the northerners who could do little but duck for cover.

By 9:00 a.m. on September 15, the Union garrison surrendered, and the Confederates took possession of 12,419 federal prisoners, 13,000 small arms, 73 artillery pieces, and 200 wagons. Casualties were relatively light: 44 Union soldiers killed and 173 wounded, with Confederate deaths totaling 39 in addition to 247 wounded in action.

Much of the land involved in the pivotal 1862 encounter, as well as in the earlier John Brown Raid, is now a part of Harpers Ferry National

Historical Park. For more information, call the park's visitor center at (304) 535-6029, or visit www.nps.gov/hafe.

Dharma Farm
High View

West Virginia may not be the first place that comes to mind when planning to build a monastery for Buddhist monks and nuns and a haven in which curious laypeople learn to meditate and become mindful.

It fit the bill, though, for the founding abbot Bhante Henepola Gunaratana, who had been working at a Buddhist center in Washington, D.C., but was looking for a more peaceful place in which to teach meditation.

The Sri Lanka–born abbot came across the initial acreage for what would become the Bhavana Society Forest Monastery in 1984, while looking for a site that was conducive to meditation, inexpensive, and relatively close to the Washington–Baltimore area.

In the eastern hills of Hampshire County, a friend found just such a place, which happened to be selling for $18,000—the exact amount the Bhavana Society had in its bank account. The monastery property has since grown to include forty-eight acres.

In addition to providing an ordination program for Buddhist monks and nuns, the Bhavana Society holds a variety of retreats on such topics as mindfulness, concentration, and insight, as well as introduction to meditation for curious laypeople. The retreats range from three to ten days and involve living simply in spartan quarters. Meals are vegetarian, and none are served after noon. Meditations are held at 5:00 a.m. and 5:30 p.m. Phones and computers should be left at home.

The cost for the retreats is unspecified. It is left to participants to calculate the appropriate tribute of generosity, or *dana,* to leave.

To visit the Bhavana Society Forest Monastery, check out www .bhavanasociety.org, or call (304) 856-3241.

Have a Blast in the Wilderness

Laneville

To many backpackers trekking through the 27 square miles of the Dolly Sods Wilderness, sweeping views of wide-open heathland rimmed with windswept red spruce trees and eerie sandstone outcroppings are to die for.

In fact, the Army Corps of Engineers has spent a lot of time, effort, and money over the years to make sure no one actually dies while taking in the scenery at West Virginia's most popular wilderness area.

Dolly Sods was pummeled with thousands of mortar and artillery shells in 1943 and 1944 when it was used as a training ground for

Dolly Sods is the only wilderness area where WARNING: LIVE BOMBS signs are posted at the trailheads.

U.S. Army troops preparing to invade Italy during World War II. Many of the high-explosive projectiles failed to detonate during the in-country training maneuvers.

Before returning the 4,000-foot-high plateau to the Monongahela National Forest at war's end, Army sappers swept the most heavily bombarded sections of the wilderness for unexploded ordnance. In 1946 Army Engineer Bomb and Shell Disposal Team No. 6 found and destroyed 189 live mortar shells and 4 live artillery rounds and declared the site to be "safe for grazing, lumbering, or hunting."

But a follow-up sweep in 1953 turned up six more live mortar shells. Subsequent sweeps with more sophisticated detection gear in the 1980s and '90s produced an additional fifty-seven unexploded mortar and artillery shells. As recently as 2005 hikers have spotted several additional live rounds, which demolition experts later detonated in place, while traveling through the 17,000-acre wilderness area.

Trails and backcountry campsites in the wilderness have been thoroughly swept for ordnance, but the area is too vast to be completely cleared of all unexploded munitions. Signs posted at all Dolly Sods trailheads carry photos of rusty mortar rounds and warn hikers and backpackers to look out for but avoid touching them.

So far, the World War II–vintage weaponry has injured only one person. In 1951 teenager Wallace Dean was hunting in the wilderness area with a friend who picked up a live mortar round, then set it down on a rock, causing it to explode. Dean suffered severe leg injuries and was unable to walk for about a year, but he eventually recovered. Dean later became an ecologist for the Army Corps of Engineers and served on the corps' project team responsible for clearing unexploded ordnance from Dolly Sods during the 1990s.

More than 50,000 people a year visit the Dolly Sods Wilderness, named for the pioneer Dahle family who grazed livestock on the highland terrain where blueberry, huckleberry, and cranberry bushes now thrive.

To enter the Dolly Sods Wilderness from Elkins, follow US 33 east to Harman, then take WV 32 north to Laneville Road (State Secondary Route 45). Follow Laneville Road east for 6 miles to Red Creek Bridge and the southwestern entrance to the wilderness area.

For more information on Dolly Sods Wilderness, visit www.fs.fed .us/r9/mnf/sp/dolly_sods_wilderness, or call the Monongahela National Forest office at (304) 636-1800.

Minnesota We're Not

Lost River

If size matters, when it comes to lakes, then West Virginia's Trout Pond may have some esteem issues.

The one-and-a-half-acre body of water in the George Washington National Forest in Hardy County is West Virginia's only natural lake.

Trout Pond, West Virginia's sole natural lake, is a place for reflection. Kenny Kemp

★ ★

While the state has several lakes more than 1,000 times larger than Trout Pond, they are all man-made reservoirs, while Trout Pond is a naturally occurring limestone sinkhole with a boulder-blocked outflow.

Trout Pond is so small, it occasionally dries up during periods of drought. While bass tournaments, water skiing—and sometimes water—won't be found at the tiny lake, visitors are welcome to fish the small, tree-lined pond, which is encircled by a hiking trail. Nearby

Bisexual Bass

There's something in the water of the South Branch of the Potomac River near this Hardy County town that makes male smallmouth bass want to get in touch with their feminine side.

In 2003 fish biologists discovered that an alarming number of male South Branch bass were developing immature eggs inside their testes. A follow-up survey in 2008 showed that nearly 80 percent of the male bass in the South Branch had begun to produce eggs.

Researchers suspect that endocrine-disrupting contaminants, such as human estrogen from processed sewage or animal estrogen from farm manure and some pesticides, may be behind the "intersex" fish phenomenon. The highest concentrations of intersex bass are found near population centers and agricultural areas.

Since 2003 the gender-bent bass have been found in the Potomac as far downstream as Washington, D.C. There is evidence that intersex fish are less resistant to disease and stress than normal fish, and the he-she fish have been victims of several fish kills. The condition has not seemed to significantly hamper smallmouth bass reproduction in the Potomac.

Rockcliff Lake, located in the U.S. Forest Service's Trout Pond Recreation Area, seems huge by comparison at seventeen acres, is a much more productive trout lake, and comes equipped with a swimming beach.

A fifty-site campground and a series of hiking trails can be found in Trout Pond Recreation Area, which encompasses both Trout Pond and Rockcliff Lake. To reach Trout Pond from the Hardy County town of Lost River, take State Secondary Route 16 (Mill Gap/Thorn Bottom Road) east for about 5 miles to its intersection with Forest Service Road 500. Turn right on Forest Service Road 500 and follow it 1.7 miles to the entrance to Trout Pond Recreation Area. For more information, call the George Washington and Thomas Jefferson National Forest headquarters at (540) 265-5100.

A Mountain of Ice Holes
North River Mills

During the dog days of summer, generations of people from the North River Mills area of Hampshire County have walked to the rocky slopes at the base of a nearby mountain looking for ice holes.

Natural vents formed between the rocks at the bottom of a large boulder field, or talus slope, on one shoulder of the mountain emit cold air at a temperature of 38 degrees Fahrenheit year-round. Inside these holes, ice can often be found in midsummer, when people familiar with the phenomenon would chip out buckets full of ice and lug them home to make hand-cranked ice cream.

The ice is formed in cooler months, when moist, cold air sinks deep into the talus, and masses of ice form inside. Some naturalists believe a permanent lens of ice lies beneath the shattered sandstone boulders, which insulate it and keep it intact. When the seasons change and the weather warms up, cold air flows out of more than sixty small vents at the bottom of Ice Mountain. The cold air creates a microclimate that sustains a number of plants usually found far to the north, such as twinflower, Canada mayflower, and bristly rose.

West Virginia Bananas

If you hear West Virginians discussing the various ways to cook and eat pawpaw, it doesn't necessarily mean they are cannibals about to make their grandfather an entree.

Pawpaws are a fruit native to the lower-elevation hardwood forests in the East and Midwest, including much of West Virginia. The green-coated, potato-shaped fruits grow in clusters on shrublike pawpaw trees, usually approaching ripeness in September. They're ripe when their skins turn dark and the fruit separates easily from the branch or falls to the ground. The pawpaw's pulpy, yellow-orange flesh has a tropical flavor, a blend of banana, mango, and vanilla custard with a slight metallic aftertaste. The flesh is also loaded with large black seeds that need to be strained before using the fruit to make bread, pies, custards, or jams.

Pawpaws have long been appreciated by people who live within their range. Early European explorers observed Native Americans eating and growing pawpaws. When the Corps of Discovery returned from its epic journey to the Pacific in 1806, William Clark wrote of spending a full day along the lower Missouri River "to let the men gather pawpaws or the custard apple of which this country abounds and the men are very fond of."

Some strains of pawpaws are now being cultivated in orchards in West Virginia's Eastern Panhandle and sold in Washington, D.C., area farmers' markets. The Morgan County town of Paw Paw gets its name from the native fruit.

★ ★

The fragile, 150-acre site is protected by the West Virginia Chapter of The Nature Conservancy, which maintains two trails on the Ice Mountain Preserve. The trails are open to guided visitation most of the year by calling (304) 496-7359 at least three weeks before the planned visit.

Bare-Bones Vacation

Paw Paw

The dress code for dinner seating at Avalon, a full-service resort in the hills of Morgan County, is pretty basic: Coat and tie are optional. So are jeans, T-shirts, tank tops, swimsuits, or any other type of clothing.

West Virginia's sole clothing-optional resort offers its guests a secluded, 250-acre expanse of wooded hills to get in touch with nature by going natural. Avalon has a lodge with hotel-style rooms, a campground, a dining room, tennis and volleyball courts, and horseshoe pits, along with a fishing lake, indoor and outdoor pools, spas, and saunas.

The resort is open year-round, with snow angel making among the featured off-season activities. Special events include Avalonfest, an outdoor music and arts festival; Starry Nights, a nude spring formal in which a prom queen and king are crowned; and a midsummer Nude Recreation Week.

For more information, visit www.avalon-resort.com, or call (304) 947-5600.

Convoy Curator

Petersburg

Gereald Bland probably doesn't waste a lot of time worrying about thieves breaking into his property on the outskirts of Petersburg.

When you have more than forty restored military vehicles on your land, along with a battery of artillery pieces, a few practice bombs, an

★ ★

What started out as a Jeep restoration hobby ended up as Top Kick's Military Museum. Lawrence Pierce

amphibious landing craft, a small arsenal of weapons, and the know-how to use them all, an intruder is likely to find an easier target.

Bland never set out to build a museum, but that's what evolved in the years that followed his decision to buy and restore a World War II–era Jeep he spotted rusting away in a West Virginia hayfield in 1982. Since then he has acquired more than twenty Jeeps, a dozen military trucks, a variety of tracked vehicles, a couple of ambulances, and a World War II Buffalo landing craft once used to carry troops from ship to shore.

"When we found something we liked and we had the money, we bought it," said Bland, who served in the army from 1949 to 1971, retiring as a first sergeant, or "top-kick." To find and acquire antique military hardware, he and his wife, Virginia, have traveled as far as Montana, where they picked up a 106-millimeter recoilless rifle, crammed it into their van, and drove it home. "We had 6 inches of room inside the van to spare," he said.

"It would be great to get a tank or a helicopter sometime," said Bland. "But when your museum operates on donations instead of admission fees, you won't get far enough ahead to buy big-ticket items like those."

In addition to weaponry and rolling stock, Top Kick's Military Museum includes exhibits of uniforms, flight suits, rations, and radio gear. The items were originally used by soldiers, both friend and foe, from the Civil War through the current conflicts in Iraq and Afghanistan.

The museum has more vehicles than it does indoor space, so many of the larger trucks are parked outside, surrounded by corn and grain fields

Bland, the museum's main tour guide as well as owner, says his main reward for showing off his collection is the favorable feedback he gets from veterans. His own military service included two tours in Vietnam, where he was a combat engineer and the recipient of a Bronze Star medal for valor and meritorious service, as well as stints in Alaska and Germany.

While the museum's existence is not heavily advertised, he has given tours to visitors from nearly all fifty states and several foreign countries. Most visitors are in the area to take in other attractions, spot the museum's billboard on WV 55, and make a spur-of-the-moment visit. The museum is open year-round, from 9:00 a.m. to dark Monday through Saturday, and noon to dark on Sundays. Admission is free, but donations are appreciated.

For more information, call (304) 257-1392, or visit www.topkicks militarymuseum.com.

Riding the Petersburg Wave
Petersburg

While West Virginia may lack a seacoast, its Petersburg Wave, which starts with a 4,000-foot plunge off the Allegheny Front, brings in hundreds of thrill-seeking visitors to Grant County each winter.

The Petersburg area is the home of one of the eastern United States' strongest and most reliable mountain waves, an atmospheric phenomenon created when a steady wind sweeps at a right angle across a mountain ridge—in this case the 4,200-foot Allegheny Front. Wind rises at the crest of the ridge, then cools and plummets into the valley formed by the South Branch of the Potomac River, which surrounds Petersburg, a few miles east of the ridgetop. In stable, steady winds, the friction between the upward and downward forces at the edge of the ridge produces an oscillation that takes the form of a mountain wave—a smooth mass of air that can generate neck-snapping lift, sometimes exceeding 1,000 feet per minute.

Glider pilots from around the world flock to the tiny Grant County Airport in February and March, when the wave is generally strongest, in hopes of attaining 5 kilometers (about 3.1 miles) of elevation gain

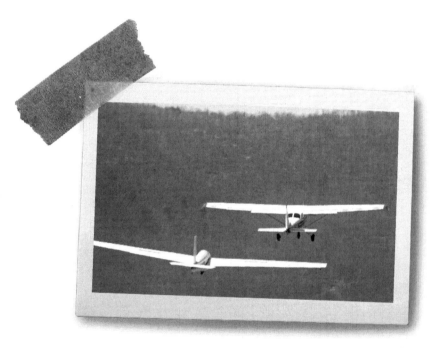

A glider gets a tow toward the Allegheny Front and the chance to use wind power to climb 20,000 feet. Kenny Kemp.

in a single flight. That's the requirement needed to receive the coveted Diamond Badge from the Fédération Aéronautique Internationale, the world governing body for air sports. A number of sailplanes riding the Petersburg Wave have climbed well past the 20,000-foot mark.

Stahl Flying Services at Grant County Airport hosts a series of wave camps in February and early March to accommodate Diamond Badge seekers with tow planes, oxygen, and a heated lounge with lots of hot food, drink, and companionship. During the wave camps, the Federal Aviation Administration grants glider pilots special permission to climb above 20,000 feet and into the airspace usually reserved for commercial traffic. Jet traffic is routed around the ascending sailplanes.

For more information on, and photos of, the Petersburg Wave Camp, go to www.stahlflyingservices.com, or call (304) 257-4435.

What a Dive!

Scherr

While West Virginia isn't known as a mecca for scuba enthusiasts, having a lake heated by burning coal draws crowds of divers from across the Northeast.

While they don't find coral reefs, sunken ships, or tropical fish beneath the surface of the 1,200-acre reservoir, divers at Mount Storm Lake do find sunken pine trees, a fence, a shed, a stream chan-nel, quarrying equipment, a motorcycle, and schools of bluegill and catfish. But mostly they find tropical water temperatures that remain at bath water levels most of the year.

A Dominion Power coal-fired generating plant on one shore of the lake burns up to 15,000 tons of coal daily and uses nearly a quarter million gallons of lake water per minute to cool its three huge gen-erating units. Water from the cooling towers is returned to the lake unnaturally warm, driving water temperatures into the mid-90s in the summer and fall, and keeping the lake in the 50- to 60-degree range in the dead of winter, when nearby lakes are frozen over.

Ramping It Up

In most other states, the word *ramps* conjures up images of freeway interchanges, wheelchair platforms, or skateboard parks. But to West Virginians ramps signal the arrival of spring and another season of festivals and feeds dedicated to the adored, odiferous Appalachian herb.

The ramp, or *Allium tricoccum,* is a member of the onion family that resembles a large leek and grows wild on upland slopes across West Virginia, where it is dug from late February to early April, depending on elevation. Once removed from the ground, the bulb emits a distinctive (some would say stinky) aroma that is only enhanced by

Pungent ramps (wild leeks) in the spring cause celebrations across West Virginia. Chris Dorst

cooking. It's the scent of money for volunteer fire departments, churches, and service clubs that rely on ramp feeds as a primary source of income.

In West Virginia ramps are often fried with potatoes in bacon grease or scrambled with eggs and served with such side dishes as ham, pinto beans, and cornbread. There are numerous festivals associated with the annual arrival of the wild leek. The largest is the annual Feast of the Ramson in Richwood in April, when more than 1 ton of the halitosis-friendly herbs are served. The festival got its start in 1938, when a group of local ramp-loving "Dignitaries" hosted the event.

Richwood is also the home of the world's only ramp farm, operated by Glen and Norene Facemire on their acreage along the South Fork of the Cherry River. The Facemires have collected seeds from wild ramps and cultivated their own homegrown strains of the plant on their forested slopes. During ramp season they clean, pack, and ship fresh ramps to expatriate Appalachians across the world.

In the 1950s Jim Comstock, the publisher of Richwood's *West Virginia Hillbilly* newspaper, ramped up his status as a local journalistic legend by printing a special Feast of the Ramson issue using ramp-scented ink. Since many copies of the *Hillbilly* were sent through the mail, a number of postal workers lodged complaints over the aromatic bulk mailing. In a photograph that appeared in an early 1950s *National Geographic* issue, Richwood postmaster Wheeler Green was shown holding his nose and reading a copy of the *Hillbilly*.

Diving clubs have built platforms at depths of 25, 50, and 90 feet within a short distance of the shore access area for divers. The lake is popular for divers working on open water certification and other training. Locals use the lake as a three-season swimming hole, often staying long into the night.

Shoreline amenities are scarce, beyond a state-maintained boat ramp and a couple of portable toilets. But use of the lake is free and open to the public.

As its name suggests, the lake, located atop a high (3,244-foot) plateau, is prone to receiving extreme weather any time of the year. While the water temperature may be cozy, the air temperatures can be cold, particularly if driven by the strong westerly winds that power a chain of wind turbines that can be seen on a ridge not far from the lake.

There is no lake office, visitor center, or contact number for Mount Storm Lake, located along WV 93, between Davis and Scherr. There are no stores or restaurants in the immediate vicinity of the lake, so stock up before arriving.

Shepherdstown Steamer
Shepherdstown

Twenty years before Robert Fulton steamed his way up the Hudson River from New York to Albany aboard the steamboat *Clermont,* onlookers watched James Rumsey ply the waters of the Potomac at Shepherdstown in his steamboat—actually, the world's first steam-powered jetboat.

While Fulton gets the credit for developing the first working steamboat, both Rumsey and another American inventor, John Fitch, each developed successful prototype steamboats in 1787. Fitch's steamboat was a relatively crude affair that used a propulsion system of linked oars on each side of the hull. Rumsey's one-cylinder steam engine powered a water pump with an intake valve that sucked river water in, then closed as the pump forced water out through a discharge pipe at the stern. The system operated on the same basic principle as the propulsion systems used in modern-day Jet Ski watercraft but produced considerably less speed. Rumsey's steam watercraft was clocked at 3 miles an hour during its Shepherdstown debut.

Shepherdstown has paid tribute to its homegrown inventor by building the Rumsey Boathouse Museum, located at the rear of the Historic Shepherdstown Museum at the corner of Princess and German Streets. Both museums are open on Saturday and Sunday only. Call (304) 876-0910. The Rumsey Monument, a tall granite spire overlooking the stretch of the Potomac Rumsey test-piloted in 1787, can be found at the end of Mill Street. Or you can make a toast to the inventor, who was also a friend of George Washington and Benjamin Franklin, at Rumsey Tavern in Shepherdstown's Clarion Hotel.

For more information, call the Shepherdstown Visitors Center at (304) 876-2786, or visit www.shepherdstownvisitorscenter.com.

Little House on the Campus

Shepherdstown

While it looks like it could be student housing for leprechauns, a two-story stone house on the edge of the Shepherd University campus was actually built in 1929 as a place for education majors to observe kids playing in a "laboratory setting."

Shepherd's 240-square-foot Little House has a kitchen with a pine hutch; a dining room with a miniature china tea set and cabinet; a living room with a stone fireplace, sofa, and piano; and two second-floor bedrooms with beds, chairs, and drapes. Ceilings are just over 5 feet high.

Little House was built by local fifth and sixth graders, supervised by nineteen student teachers, after an area stonemason built the framework for the super-size dollhouse. Local suppliers donated building materials. While the tiny structure has not been used by Shepherd's education program for years, it is occasionally opened to visitors, often in the hours preceding home football games and on major

Beeline for Boston

When the Continental Congress called on settlers in what is now West Virginia to join the fight against the British Army following the April 19, 1775, Battle of Lexington, they didn't have to rely on sign-up bonuses, tuition payments, or cool uniforms to lure enlistees. Many able-bodied men in the Shepherdstown area had already gathered up arms and supplies in preparation for battle when the request for two companies of frontier riflemen arrived.

One of the companies, organized by Hugh Stephenson, drilled on a vacant lot behind the Entler Tavern, a building that now houses the Historic Shepherdstown Museum. The other, led by Daniel Morgan, trained at nearby Winchester. Both had orders to proceed to Boston as soon as possible to help fellow Virginian George Washington resist the Redcoats. Morgan and Stephenson each wanted to reach Boston first to prove their leadership abilities to Washington. Morgan apparently departed a few days earlier than he had planned and bypassed an agreed-upon rendezvous with Stephenson and his men in Frederick, Maryland, to beat the Shepherdstown area man to Massachusetts. When Stephenson arrived in Frederick and found out that Morgan had jumped the gun and gone on without waiting, he urged his men to march faster.

What ensued for Stephenson and his men was the Beeline March, a 600-mile trek completed in only twenty-four days, in an era of poor roads and scarce supplies. The Shepherdstown riflemen, who hoofed up to 36 miles a day, came within hours of catching their rivals from Winchester and earned personal praise from Washington when they arrived for duty.

Altogether, seven companies of Continental Army troops were raised in what is now Jefferson County, West Virginia, during the

Revolutionary War. Shepherdstown, with a population of about 1,000 at that time, was the county's largest city and is believed by some historians to have supplied more soldiers, per capita, than any other town in America during the war. Of the 300 Jefferson County enlisted men who joined the Continental Army, only about 100 are known to have survived the war.

Members of Stephenson's rifle company enjoyed a barbecue at a spring just south of Shepherdstown a few days before beginning their epic Beeline March. Those attending the cookout pledged to meet on the same date, at the same place, in fifty years, assuming they survived the war and what life dealt them afterward. Only two of the original ninety-seven riflemen turned up for the reunion in 1825.

★ ★

Shepherd University education majors once studied
children at play in this tiny "laboratory."

holidays. The house is located on North Princess Street, a half block
off German Street, Shepherdstown's main drag.

For more information, call the Shepherdstown Visitors Center at
(304) 876-2786, or visit www.shepherdstownvisitorscenter.com.

Room with a Pew

Silver Lake

While religion is a big part of West Virginia's social fabric, Our Lady of
the Pines Catholic Church in the tiny community of Silver Lake urges
its visitors to think small. The 12-foot-wide, 24-foot-long church with
seating for no more than twelve bills itself as the "Smallest Church in
Forty-eight States," according to a sign outside the building.

Built in 1958 by Lithuanian immigrant Peter L. Milkint as a tribute
to his parents, the church has stained-glass windows, a brick exterior,
and six pews, each capable of holding no more than two adults.

Used mainly for weddings (it can hold twenty-four people, standing room only), the church attracts tens of thousands of visitors annually who are interested in its miniature size.

Admission to Our Lady of the Pines is free, although donations are appreciated. The church is located a few yards off US 219 in the Tucker County town of Silver Lake. There is no phone or Web site. Our Lady of the Pines is open daily, from daylight to dusk, weather permitting.

Big Brother's Listening Post?
Sugar Grove

While West Virginia lacks a seacoast, the decidedly unsalty waters of the South Fork of the South Branch of the Potomac River run through the state's only Navy base, the Naval Information Operations Command facility at Sugar Grove.

A Navy base keeps a low profile in the West Virginia highlands.
Lawrence Pierce

Byrd Houses

What one taxpayer may view as a wasteful government "pork barrel" project, another may consider a valuable economic development tool.

No matter the point of view, Senator Robert C. Byrd is the undisputed king of bringing home the bacon when it comes to earmarking federal public works projects for his home state.

In 1990, two years after being named chairman of the Senate Appropriations Committee, Byrd declared his intention to become a "billion-dollar industry" for West Virginia. He ended up underestimating his pull when it came to serving up the pork. By the end of 2008, he had brought $3.3 billion worth of federal construction and development spending to the Mountain State.

This federal courthouse in Charleston is one of many tributes to Robert C. Byrd's edifice complex.

As a result, West Virginia's landscape is dappled with what one taxpayer group terms "Other White Meat" developments named in honor of the state's senior senator.

Here's a recent listing:

Robert C. Byrd Telescope at the National Radio Astronomy Observatory, Green Bank

Robert C. Byrd Academic and Technology Center, South Charleston

Robert C. Byrd Addition to Oglebay Resort's lodge, Wheeling

Robert C. Byrd Bridge, Huntington

Robert. C. Byrd Biotechnology Science Center, Huntington

Robert C. Byrd Clinical Addition to Veterans Administration Hospital, Huntington

Robert C. Byrd Community Center, Pine Grove

Robert C. Byrd Community Center, Sugar Grove

Robert C. Byrd Drive, Beckley

Robert C. Byrd Expressway, Weirton

Robert C. Byrd Highway, Appalachian Corridor H between Weston and Wardensville

Robert C. Byrd Freeway, Appalachian Corridor G between Williamson and Charleston

Robert C. Byrd Interchange, US 19, Birch River

Robert C. Byrd U.S. Courthouse and Federal Building, Beckley

Robert C. Byrd U.S. Courthouse and Federal Building, Charleston

Robert C. Byrd Hardwood Technologies Center, Princeton

(Continued)

Robert C. Byrd Health Sciences Center of West Virginia, Morgantown, and Charleston

Robert C. Byrd High School, Clarksburg

Robert C. Byrd Hilltop Office Complex, Rocket City

Robert C. Byrd Industrial Park, Paw Paw

Robert C. Byrd Institute, Charleston

Robert C. Byrd Institute for Advanced Flexible Manufacturing, Huntington

Robert C. Byrd Learning Resource Center, Beckley

Robert C. Byrd Library, Beckley

Robert C. Byrd Locks and Dam, Apple Grove

Robert C. Byrd National Technology Transfer Center, Wheeling

Robert C. Byrd Rural Health Center, Huntington

Robert C. Byrd Science Center, Shepherdstown

Robert C. Byrd Technology Center, Philippi

Robert C. Byrd Visitor Center, Harpers Ferry

The Navy's presence in this remote corner of the state, surrounded by the George Washington National Forest and bracketed by 4,000-foot-high Allegheny Mountain ridges, dates to 1955. That was the year the site was selected by the Naval Research Laboratory for an "advanced communications research" facility. Plans called for the installation of a radio telescope with a 600-foot parabolic antenna at the base of Shenandoah Mountain, allowing operators to tune into radio signals as far as thirty-eight billion light years away.

While the Navy built a 60-foot antenna to test the feasibility of the larger scope, advances in technology made the original premise for developing a 600-foot dish obsolete. Enter Robert C. Byrd (see "Byrd Houses" sidebar) with a request to find a new use for the only active-duty military base in his home state. In 1968 the Navy decided to take advantage of the newly designated National Radio Quiet Zone (see "13,000 Miles of Quiet") and build a 150-foot parabolic dish antenna to serve as the main receiver for worldwide Navy communications coming into the Washington, D.C., area.

By the end of the 1960s, two huge, 1,000-foot-diameter Wullen-weber antenna arrays were built to augment the 150-foot receiver, and the hush-hush Naval Security Group had established a presence at the base. In 1992 the base officially became a Naval Security Group Activity.

In a 2005 article in the *New York Times,* the small West Virginia Navy base with its array of parabolic dishes was described as "the country's largest eavesdropping bug," capable of "secretly and silently seeping in millions of private telephone calls and e-mail messages an hour." According to the article, the base at Sugar Grove is run by the ultrasecret National Security Agency and intercepts "all international communications entering the eastern United States."

The same year the *New York Times* piece appeared, the Sugar Grove facility became a part of the Navy Information Operations Command. The NIOC, among other duties, has taken over the "cryptologic element responsibilities" previously performed by the Naval Security Group, according to the base's Web site.

The base is the home to about 200 members of the "Mountaineer Navy," as sailors serving at Sugar Grove call themselves. The base has its own bowling alley, gym, remote rental cabins, pool, racquetball courts, and hobby shop. Base officials frequently win awards for environmental stewardship and work with the state Division of Natural Resources to protect rare plants known to grow on the installation.

★ ★

According to a statement posted on the home page of the base's Web site (www.nnwc-ftmeade.navy.mil/SugarGrove), the mission of NIOC Sugar Grove is "to conduct communications research and development for the Department of the Navy, the Department of Defense, and other U.S. government agencies."

The Collossi of Unger
Unger

Top the last hill along Winchester Grade Road before hitting the Virginia border just south of the Morgan County community of Unger, and you'll see redbud and apple trees, cattle grazing in pastures and . . . a roller coaster holding huge statues of all five members of the Simpsons?

Welcome to Farnham's Fantasy Farm, home of more than twenty fiberglass statues between 6 and 25 feet tall, in addition to the five-car roller coaster and 160 feet of steel track that holds Homer, Marge, Bart, Lisa, and Maggie Simpson.

Standing sentinel at the end of George and Pam Farnham's driveway are the largest of the Unger Collossi. There's Brian the Beach Guy, a 25-foot-tall fiberglass figure of a surfer dude in swim trunks holding a can of Coke, who once towered over an upstate New York amusement park. Next to him is Biker Babe "BB" Queen, a 17-foot-tall bikini-clad hottie with three tattoos, who once worked as a Uniroyal Tire promoter in Mississippi. A huge fiberglass arm's-length away is a 25-foot-tall Midas Muffler man, imported from California a few years ago, the Farnham's senior statue. Then there's Big John the Grocery Guy, a 23-foot-tall checkout man, who once towered over a southern Illinois supermarket, as well as a 19-foot Santa from a Dallas shopping mall.

Scattered about the Fantasy Farm's seven acres are an assortment of smaller statues, including a pterodactyl from a New Jersey miniature golf course, a 21-foot-tall former Muffler Man who has been converted into a Paul Bunyan from Florida, and 6-foot-tall likenesses of *Yogi Bear Show* characters Ranger Smith and Cindy Bear from a Michigan campground.

Behind the collection of fiberglass statues, a small herd of llamas and alpacas grazes in a pasture.

The Farnhams are full-time dealers of smaller collectibles—things like vintage books, pinup calendars, figurines, and amusement park tourist schlock—that they sell on eBay or in an antique mall in nearby Berkeley Springs.

"When our house filled up with the little stuff we collect, we decided to collect bigger stuff outside," says George Farnham, a former attorney. "Now, we own seven of the nine giant fiberglass statues in West Virginia. . . . Thank God for no zoning in Morgan County!"

While the Farnham Fantasy Farm is not exactly set up for tourists (its only amenity is a larger than normal parking lot), visitors are welcome to stop by and look around.

"You can't put stuff like this out in your yard and not expect people to stop," Farnham says.

To reach Farnham Fantasy Farm from Berkeley Springs, take US 522 south about 2 miles to the junction with Winchester Grade Road/State Secondary Route 13. Turn left on Winchester Grade Road and follow it south about 7 miles until you see the giant figures on the left. The Farnhams can be reached by e-mail at animalfa@ix.netcom .com.

index

index

index

index

about the author

A reporter and feature writer for the *Charleston Gazette* for more than 30 years, Rick Steelhammer has traveled by car, plane, helicopter, raft, canoe, kayak, train, speeder car, horse, skis, snowshoes, zipline, and on foot to file multiple stories from each of West Virginia's fifty-five counties. He also writes a weekly humor column for the *Sunday Gazette-Mail*, which the National Society of Newspaper Columnists once judged to be the second-best in the nation among large-circulation newspapers.